# Hans Christian Andersen

## His most beloved fairy tales

*This book belongs to:*

Hans Christian Andersen – his most beloved fairy tales
Author: Hans Christian Andersen

ISBN: 978-87-7884-534-4
Globe Publishing

Illustrations: Sidsel Brix
English translation:
Jean Hersholt
Editor: Lars Serritslev
Assistant editor: Louise Buckens
DTP: Jannik Kristensen
1. edition, 1. printing


Globe Publishing • Skodsborgvej 305 D • 2850 Nærum • Denmark
Phone: +45 70151400 • Fax: +45 70151410
www.globe-publishing.com • info@globe-publishing.com
Printed in Hungary, 2014

# Hans Christian Andersen

## His most beloved fairy tales

# Contents

# Foreword

In this book, we have gathered a collection Hans Christian Andersen's most beloved and timeless fairy tales. The Danish storyteller's multidimensional universe provides a great insight into humanity and continues to capture readers of all ages and cultures. The stories and their content will always be relevant. The fairy tales provide a beautiful occasion to read out loud to children, who will no doubt be captivated by the stories as well as by the colourful and playful illustrations of Sidsel Brix.

*- The Editors*

*About the illustrator:*

Sidsel Brix is a Danish illustrator, educated at the design school in Kolding in 2005. "From an early age, I have always had a special relationship to the fairy tales of Hans Christian Andersen. The images of those fairy tales have been engrained in me from childhood and when I became an illustrator, it was with the wish of drawing for children and with children. I love moving in the universe of the child, where everything is so straightforward and yet so complex. It is with my greatest pleasure that I have been allowed to express my inner images and thoughts about the fairy tales that I love so dearly. I hope you will enjoy moving in this universe as much I have done."

*- Sidsel Brix, illustrator*

# The Tinderbox

There came a soldier marching down the high road-one, two! one, two! He had his knapsack on his back and his sword at his side as he came home from the wars. On the road he met a witch, an ugly old witch, a witch whose lower lip dangled right down on her chest.

"Good evening, soldier," she said. "What a fine sword you've got there, and what a big knapsack. Aren't you every inch a soldier! And now you shall have money, as much as you please."

"That's very kind, you old witch," said the soldier.

"See that big tree." The witch pointed to one near by them. "It's hollow to the roots. Climb to the top of the trunk and you'll find a hole through which you can let yourself down deep under the tree. I'll tie a rope around your middle, so that when you call me I can pull you up again."

"What would I do deep down under that tree?" the soldier wanted to know.

"Fetch money," the witch said. "Listen. When you touch bottom you'll find yourself in a great hall. It is very bright there, because more than a hundred lamps are burning. By their light you will see three doors. Each door has a key in it, so you can open them all.

"If you walk into the first room, you'll see a large chest in the middle of the floor. On it sits a dog, and his eyes are as big as saucers. But don't worry about that. I'll give you my blue checked apron to spread out on the floor. Snatch up that dog and set him on my apron. Then you can open the chest and take out as many pieces of money as you please. They are all copper.

"But if silver suits you better, then go into the next room. There sits a dog and his eyes are as big as mill wheels. But don't you care about that. Set the dog on my apron while you line your pockets with silver.

"Maybe you'd rather have gold. You can, you know. You can have all the gold you can carry if you go into the third room. The only hitch is that there on the money-chest sits a dog, and each of his eyes is as big as the Round Tower of Copenhagen.

That's the sort of dog he is. But never you mind how fierce he looks. Just set him on my apron and he'll do you no harm as you help yourself from the chest to all the gold you want." "That suits me," said the soldier. "But what do you get out of all this, you old witch? I suppose that you want your share."

"No indeed," said the witch. "I don't want a penny of it. All I ask is for you to fetch me an old tinderbox that my grandmother forgot the last time she was down there."

"Good," said the soldier. "Tie the rope around me."

"Here it is," said the witch, "and here's my blue checked apron."

The soldier climbed up to the hole in the tree and let himself slide through it, feet foremost down into the great hall where the hundreds of lamps were burning, just as the witch had said. Now he threw open the first door he came to. Ugh! There sat a dog glaring at him with eyes as big as saucers.

"You're a nice fellow," the soldier said, as he shifted him to the witch's apron and took all the coppers that his pockets would hold. He shut up the chest, set the dog back on it, and made for the second room. Alas and alack! There sat the dog with eyes as big as mill wheels.

"Don't you look at me like that." The soldier set him on the witch's apron. "You're apt to strain your eyesight." When he saw the chest brimful of silver, he threw away all his coppers and

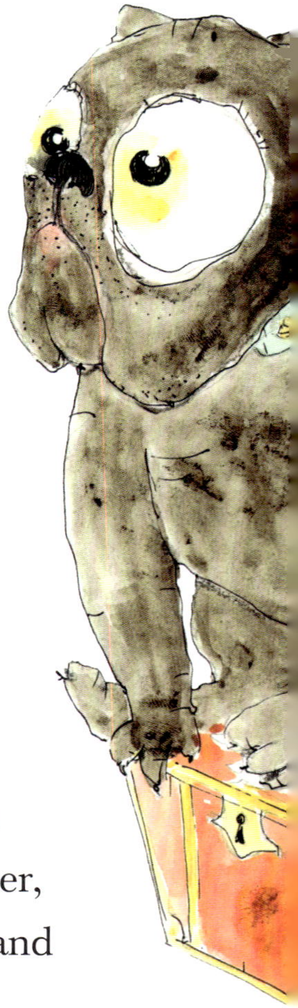

filled both his pockets and knapsack with silver alone. Then he went into the third room. Oh, what a horrible sight to see! The dog in there really did have eyes as big as the Round Tower, and when he rolled them they spun like wheels.

"Good evening," the soldier said, and saluted, for such a dog he had never seen before. But on second glance he thought to himself, "This won't do." So he lifted the dog down to the floor, and threw open the chest. What a sight! Here was gold and to spare. He could buy out all Copenhagen with it. He could buy all the cake-woman's sugar pigs, and all the tin soldiers, whips, and rocking horses there are in the world. Yes, there was really money!

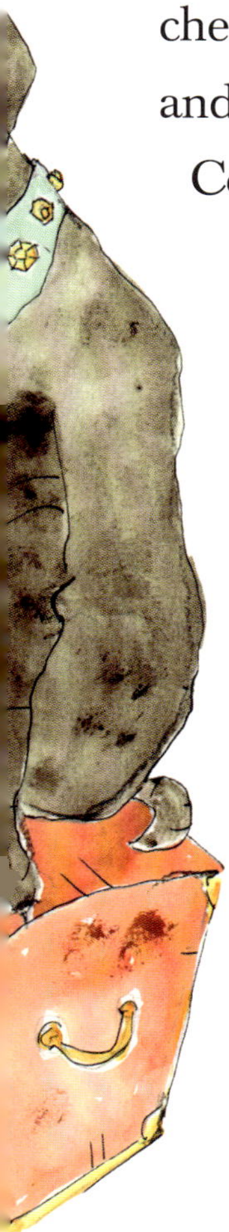

In short order the soldier got rid of all the silver coins he had stuffed in his pockets and knapsack, to put gold in their place. Yes sir, he crammed all his pockets, his knapsack, his cap, and his boots so full that he scarcely could walk. Now he was made of money. Putting the dog back on the chest he banged out the door and called up through the hollow tree:

"Pull me up now, you old witch."

"Have you got the tinderbox?" asked the witch.

"Confound the tinderbox," the soldier shouted. "I clean forgot it."

When he fetched it, the witch hauled him up. There he stood on the highroad again, with his pockets, boots, knapsack and cap full of gold.

"What do you want with the tinderbox?" he asked the old witch.

"None of your business," she told him.

"You've had your money, so hand over my tinderbox."

"Nonsense," said the soldier. "I'll take out my sword and I'll cut your head off if you don't tell me at once what you want with it."

"I won't," the witch screamed at him.

So he cut her head off. There she lay! But he tied all his money in her apron, slung it over his shoulder, stuck the tinderbox in his pocket, and struck out for town. It was a splendid town. He took the best rooms at the best inn, and ordered all the good things he liked to eat, for he was a rich man now because he had so much money. The servant who cleaned his boots may have thought them remarkably well worn for a man of such means, but that was before he went shopping. Next morning he bought boots worthy of him, and the best clothes. Now that he had turned out to be such a fashionable gentleman, people told him all about the splendors of their town-all about their King, and what a pretty Princess he had for a daughter.

"Where can I see her?" the soldier inquired.

"You can't see her at all," everyone said. "She lives in a great copper castle inside all sorts of walls and towers. Only the King can come in or go out of it, for it's been foretold that the Princess will marry a common soldier. The King would much rather she didn't."

"I'd like to see her just the same," the soldier thought. But there was no way to manage it,

Now he lived a merry life. He went to the theatre, drove about in the

King's garden, and gave away money to poor people. This was to his credit, for he remembered from the old days what it feels like to go without a penny in your pocket. Now that he was wealthy and - well dressed, he had all too many who called him their friend and a genuine gentleman. That pleased him

But he spent money every day without making any, and wound up with only two coppers to his name. He had to quit his fine quarters to live in a garret, clean his own boots, and mend them himself with a darning needle. None of his friends came to see him, because there were too many stairs to climb.

One evening when he sat in the dark without even enough money to buy a candle, he suddenly remembered there was a candle end in the tinderbox that he had picked up when the witch sent him down the hollow tree. He got out the tinderbox, and the moment he struck sparks from the flint of it his door burst open and there stood a dog from down under the tree. It was the one with eyes as big as saucers.

"What," said the dog, "is my lord's command?"

"What's this?" said the soldier. "Have I got the sort of tinderbox that will get me whatever I want? Go get me some money," he ordered the dog. Zip! The dog was gone. Zip! He was back again, with a bag full of copper in his mouth.

Now the soldier knew what a remarkable tinderbox he had. Strike

it once and there was the dog from the chest of copper coins. Strike it twice and here came the dog who had the silver. Three times brought the dog who guarded gold.

Back went the soldier to his comfortable quarters. Out strode the soldier in fashionable clothes. Immediately his friends knew him again, because they liked him so much.

Then the thought occurred to him, "Isn't it odd that no one ever gets to see the Princess? They say she's very pretty, but what's the good of it as long as she stays locked up in that large copper castle with so many towers? Why can't I see her? Where's my tinderbox?" He struck a light and, zip! came the dog with eyes as big as saucers.

"It certainly is late," said the soldier. "Practically midnight. But I do want a glimpse of the Princess, if only for a moment." Out the door went the dog, and before the soldier could believe it, here came the dog with the Princess on his back. She was sound asleep, and so pretty that everyone could see she was a Princess. The soldier couldn't keep from kissing her, because he was every inch a soldier. Then the dog took the Princess home.

Next morning when the King and Queen were drinking their tea, the Princess told them about the strange dream she'd had all about a dog and a soldier. She'd ridden on the dog's back, and the soldier had kissed her.

"Now that was a fine story," said the Queen. The next night one of the old ladies of the court was under orders to sit by the Princess's bed,

and see whether this was a dream or something else altogether. The soldier was longing to see the pretty Princess again, so the dog came by night to take her up and away as fast as he could run. But the old lady pulled on her storm boots and ran right after them. When she saw them disappear into a large house she thought, "Now I know where it is," and drew a big cross on the door with a piece of chalk. Then she went home to bed, and before long the dog brought the Princess home too. But when the dog saw that cross marked on the soldier's front door, he got himself a piece of chalk and cross-marked every door in the town. This was a clever thing to do, because now the old lady couldn't tell the right door from all the wrong doors he had marked.

Early in the morning along came the King and the Queen, the old lady, and all the officers, to see where the Princess had been.

"Here it is," said the King when he saw the first cross mark.

"No, my dear. There it is," said the Queen who was looking next door.

"Here's one, there's one, and yonder's another one!" said they all.

Wherever they looked they saw chalk marks, so they gave up searching.

The Queen, though, was an uncommonly clever woman, who could do more than ride in a coach. She took her big gold scissors, cut out a piece of silk, and made a neat little bag. She filled it with fine buckwheat flour and tied it on to the Princess's back. Then she pricked a little hole in it so that the flour would sift out along the way, wherever the Princess might go.

Again the dog came in the night, took the Princess on his back, and ran with her to the soldier, who loved her so much that he would have been glad to be a Prince just so he could make his wife. The dog didn't notice how the flour made a trail from

the castle ri
window, whe
with the Princ
it was all too p
Queen just whe
been.

They took the s and they put him in prison. There he sat. It was dark, and it was dismal, and they told him, "Tomorrow is the day for you to hang." That didn't cheer him up any, and as for his tinderbox he'd left it behind at the inn. In the morning he could see through his narrow little window how the people all hurried out of town to see him hanged. He heard the drums beat and he saw the soldiers march. In the crowd of running people he saw a shoemaker's boy in a leather apron and slippers.

The boy galloped so fast that off flew one slipper, which hit the wall right where the soldier pressed his face to the iron bars.

"Hey there, you shoemaker's boy, there's no hurry," the soldier shouted. "Nothing can happen till I get there. But if you run to where I live and bring me my tinderbox, I'll give you four coppers. Put your best foot foreward."

The shoemaker's boy could use four coppers, so he rushed the tinderbox to the soldier, and - well, now we shall hear what happened!

Outside the town a high gallows had been built. Around it stood soldiers and many hundred thousand people. The King and Queen sat on a splendid throne, opposite the judge and the whole council. The soldier already stood upon the ladder, but just as they were about to put the rope around his neck he said the custom was to grant a poor criminal one last small favour. He wanted to smoke a pipe of tobacco-the last he'd be smoking in this world.

The King couldn't refuse him, so the soldier struck fire from his tinderbox, once-twice-and a third time. Zip! There stood all the dogs, one with eyes as big as saucers, one with eyes as big as mill wheels, one with eyes as big as the Round Tower of Copenhagen. "Help me. Save me from hanging!" said the soldier. Those dogs took the judges and all the council, some by the leg and some by the nose, and tossed them so high that they came down broken to bits.

"Don't!" cried the King, but the biggest dog took him and the Queen too, and tossed them up after the others. Then the soldiers trembled and the people shouted, "Soldier, be our King and marry the pretty Princess."

So they put the soldier in the King's carriage. All three of his dogs danced in front of it, and shouted "Hurrah!" The boys whistled through their fingers, and the soldiers saluted. The Princess came out of the copper castle to be Queen, and that suited her exactly. The wedding lasted all of a week, and the three dogs sat at the table, with their eyes opened wider than ever before.

# The Shepherdess and the Chimneysweep

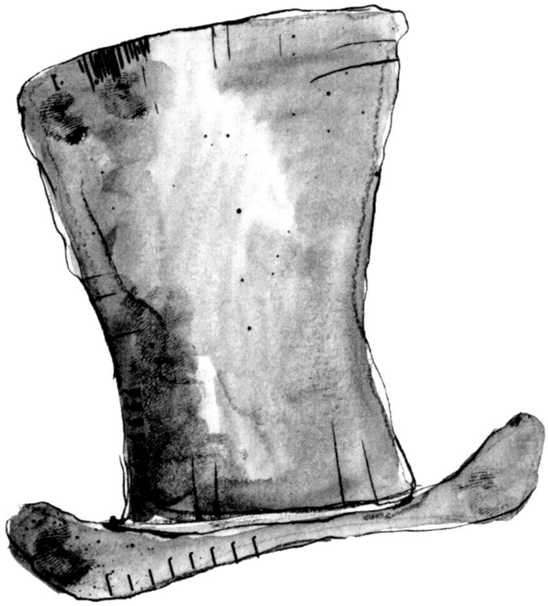

Have you ever seen a very old chest, black with age, and covered with outlandish carved ornaments and curling leaves? Well, in a certain parlour there was just such a chest, handed down from some great-grandmother. Carved all up and down it, ran tulips and roses-odd-looking flourishes-and from fanciful thickets little stags stuck out their antlered heads.

Right in the middle of the chest a whole man was carved. He made you laugh to look at him grinning away, though one couldn't call his grinning laughing. He had hind legs like a goat's, little horn on his forehead, and a long beard. All his children called him "General Headquarters-Hindquarters-Gives-Orders-Front-and-Rear-Sergeant-Billygoat-Legs." It was a difficult name to pronounce

and not many people get to be called by it, but he must have been very important or why should anyone have taken trouble to carve him at all? However, there he stood, forever eyeing a delightful little china shepherdess on the table top under the mirror. The little shepherdess wore golden shoes, and looped up her gown fetchingly with a red rose. Her hat was gold, and even her crook was gold. She was simply charming!

Close by her stood a little chimneysweep, as black as coal, but made of porcelain too. He was as clean and tidy as anyone can be, because you see he was only an ornamental chimneysweep. If the china-makers had wanted to, they could just as easily have turned him out as a prince, for he had a jaunty way of holding his ladder, and his cheeks were as pink as a girl's. That was a mistake, don't you think? He should have been dabbed with a pinch or two of soot.

He and the shepherdess stood quite close together. They had both been put on the table where they stood and, having been placed there, they had become engaged because they suited each other exactly. Both were young, both were made of the same porcelain, and neither could stand a shock.

Near them stood another figure, three times as big as they were. It was an old Chinaman who could nod his head. He too was made of porcelain, and he said he was the little shepherdess's grandfather. But he couldn't prove it.

Nevertheless he claimed that this gave him authority over her, and when General-Headquarters-Hindquarters-Gives-Orders-Front-and-Rear-Sergeant-Billygoat-Legs asked for her hand in marriage, the old Chinaman had nodded consent.

"There's a husband for you!" the old Chinaman told the shepherdess. "A husband who, I am inclined to believe, is made of mahogany. He can make you Mrs. General-Headquarters-Hindquarters-Gives-Orders-Front-and-Rear-Sergeant-Billygoat-Legs. He has the whole chest full of silver, and who knows what else he's got hidden away in his secret drawers?"

"But I don't want to go and live in the dark chest," said the little shepherdess. "I have heard people say he's got eleven china wives in there already."

"Then you will make twelve," said the Chinaman. "Tonight, as soon as the old chest commences to creak I'll marry you off to him, as sure as I'm a Chinaman." Then he nodded off to sleep. The little shepherdess cried and looked at her true love, the porcelain chimneysweep. "Please let's run away into the big, wide world," she begged him, "for we can't stay here."

"I'll do just what you want me to," the little chimneysweep told her. "Let's run away right now. I feel sure I can support you by chimney-sweeping."

"I wish we were safely down off this table," she said. "I'll never be happy until we are out in the big, wide world."

He told her not to worry, and showed her how to drop her little feet over the table edge, and how to step from one gilded leaf to another down the carved leg of the table. He set up his ladder to help her, and down they came safely to the floor. But when they glanced at the old chest they saw a great commotion. All the carved stags were craning their necks, tossing their antlers, and turning their heads. General-Headquarters-Hindquarters-Gives-Orders-Front-and -Rear-Sergeant-Billygoat-Legs jumped high in the air, and shouted to the old Chinaman, "They're running away! They're running away!" This frightened them so that they jumped quickly into a drawer of the window-seat. Here they found three or four decks of cards, not quite complete,

and a little puppet theatre, which was set up as well as it was possible to do. A play was in progress, and all the diamond queens, heart queens, club queens, and spade queens sat in front row and fanned themselves with the tulips they held in their hands. Behind them the knaves lined up, showing that they had heads both at the top and at the bottom, as face cards do have. The play was all about two people, who were not allowed to marry, and it made the shepherdess cry because it was so like her own story.

"I can't bear to see any more," she said. "I must get out of this drawer at once." But when they got back to the floor and looked up at the table, they saw the old Chinaman´s was wide awake now. Not only his head, but his whole body rocked forward. The lower part of his body was one solid piece, you see.

"The old Chinaman´s coming!" cried the little Shepherdess, who was so upset that she fell down on her porcelain knees.

"I have an idea," said the chimney-sweeper. "We'll hide in the pot-pourri vase in the corner. There we can rest upon rose petals and lavender, and when he finds us we can throw salt in his eyes."

"It's no use," she said. "Besides, I know the pot-pourri vase was once the old Chinaman´s sweetheart, and where there used to be love a little affection is sure to remain. No, there's nothing for us to do but to run away into the big wide world."

"Are you really so brave that you'd go into the wide world with me?" asked the chimneysweep. "Have you thought about how big it is, and that we can never come back here?"

"I have," she said.

The chimneysweep looked her straight in the face and said, "My way lies up through the chimney. Are you really so brave that you'll come with me into the stove, and crawl through the stovepipe? It will take us to the chimney. Once we get there, I'll know what to do. We shall climb so high that they'll never catch us, and at the very top there's an opening into the big wide world."

He led her to the stove door.

"It looks very black in there," she said. But she let him lead her through the stove and through the stovepipe, where it was pitch-black night.

"Now we've come to the chimney," he said. "And see! See how the bright star shines over our heads."

A real star, high up in the heavens, shone down as if it wished to show them the way. They clambered and scuffled, for it was hard climbing and terribly steep - way, way up high! But he lifted her up, held her safe, and found the best places for her little porcelain feet. At last they

reached the top of the chimney, where they sat down. For they were so tired, and no wonder!

Overhead was the starry sky, and spread before them were all the housetops in the town. They looked out on the big wide world. The poor shepherdess had never thought it would be like that. She flung her little head against the chimneysweep, and sobbed so many tears that the gilt washed off her sash.

"This is too much," she said. "I can't bear it. The wide world is too big. Oh! If I only were back on my table under the mirror. I'll never be happy until I stand there again, just as before. I followed you faithfully out

into the world, and if you love me the least bit you'll take me right home."

The chimneysweep tried to persuade her that it wasn't sensible to go back. He talked to her about the old Chinaman, and of General-Headquarters-Hindquarters-Gives-Orders-Front-and-Rear-Sergeant-Billygoat-Legs, but she sobbed so hard and kissed her chimneysweep so much that he had to do as she said, though he thought it was the wrong thing to do.

So back down the chimney they climbed with great difficulty, and they crawled through the wretched stovepipe into the dark stove. Here they listened behind the door, to find out what was happening in the room. Everything seemed quiet, so they opened the door and-oh, what a pity! There on the floor lay the Chinaman, in three pieces. When he had come running after them, he tumbled off the table and smashed. His whole back had come off in one piece, and his head had rolled into the corner. General-Headquarters-Hindquarters-Gives-Orders-Front-and-Rear-Sergeant-Billygoat-Legs was standing where he always stood, looking thoughtful.

"Oh, dear," said the little shepherdess, "poor old grandfather is all broken up, and it's entirely our fault. I shall never live through it." She wrung her delicate hands.

"He can be patched," said the chimneysweep. "He can be riveted. Don't be so upset about him. A little glue for his back and a strong rivet in his neck, and he will be just as good as new, and just as disagreeable as he was before."

"Will he, really?" she asked, as they climbed back to their old place on the table.

"Here we are," said the chimney-sweep. "Back where we started from. We could have saved ourselves a lot of trouble."

"Now if only old grandfather were mended," said the little shepherdess. "Is mending terribly expensive?"

He was mended well enough. The family had his back glued together, and a strong rivet put through his neck. That made him as good as new, except that never again could he nod his head.

"It seems to me that you have grown haughty since your fall, though I don't see why you should be proud of it," General-Headquarters-Hindquarters-Gives-Orders-Front-and-Rear-Sergeant-Billygoat-Legs complained. "Am I to have her, or am I not?"

The chimney-sweep and the little shepherdess looked so pleadingly at the old Chinaman, for they were deathly afraid he would nod. But he didn't. He couldn't. And neither did he care to tell anyone that, forever and a day, he'd have to wear a rivet in his neck.

So the little porcelain people remained together. They thanked goodness for the rivet in grandfather's neck, and they kept on loving each other until the day they broke.

# The Emperor's New Clothes

Once upon a time there was an Emperor so exceedingly fond of new clothes that he spent all his money on being well dressed. He cared nothing about reviewing his soldiers, going to the theatre, or going for a ride in his carriage, except to show off his new clothes. He had a coat for every hour of the day, and instead of saying, as one might, about any other ruler, "The King's in council," here they always said. "The Emperor's in his dressing room."

In the great city where he lived, life was always gay. Every day many strangers came to town, and among them one day came two swindlers. They let it be known they were weavers, and they said they could weave the most magnificent fabrics imaginable. Not only were their colours and patterns uncommonly fine, but clothes made of this cloth had a wonderful way of becoming invisible to anyone who was unfit for his office, or who was unusually stupid.

"Those would be just the clothes for me," thought the Emperor. "If I wore them I would be able to discover which men in my empire are unfit for their posts. And I could tell the wise men from the fools. Yes, I certainly must get some of the stuff woven for me right away." He paid the two swindlers a large sum of money to start work at once.

They set up two looms and pretended to weave, though there was nothing on the looms. All the finest silk and the purest old thread which they demanded went into their traveling bags, while they worked the empty looms far into the night.

"I'd like to know how those weavers are getting on with the cloth," the Emperor thought, but he felt slightly uncomfortable when he remembered that those who were unfit for their position would not be able to see the fabric. It couldn't have been that he doubted himself, yet he thought he'd rather send someone else to see how things were going. The whole town knew about the cloth's peculiar power, and all were impatient to find out how stupid their neighbors were.

"I'll send my honest old minister to the weavers," the Emperor decided. "He'll be the best one to tell me how the material looks, for he's a sensible man and no one does his duty better."

So the honest old minister went to the room where the two swindlers sat working away at their empty looms.

"Heaven help me," he thought as his eyes flew wide open, "I can't see anything at all". But he did not say so.

Both the swindlers begged him to be so kind as to come near to approve the excellent pattern, the beautiful colours. They pointed to the empty looms, and the poor old minister stared as hard as he dared. He couldn't see anything, because there was nothing to see. "Heaven have mercy," he thought. "Can it be that I'm a fool? I'd have never guessed it, and

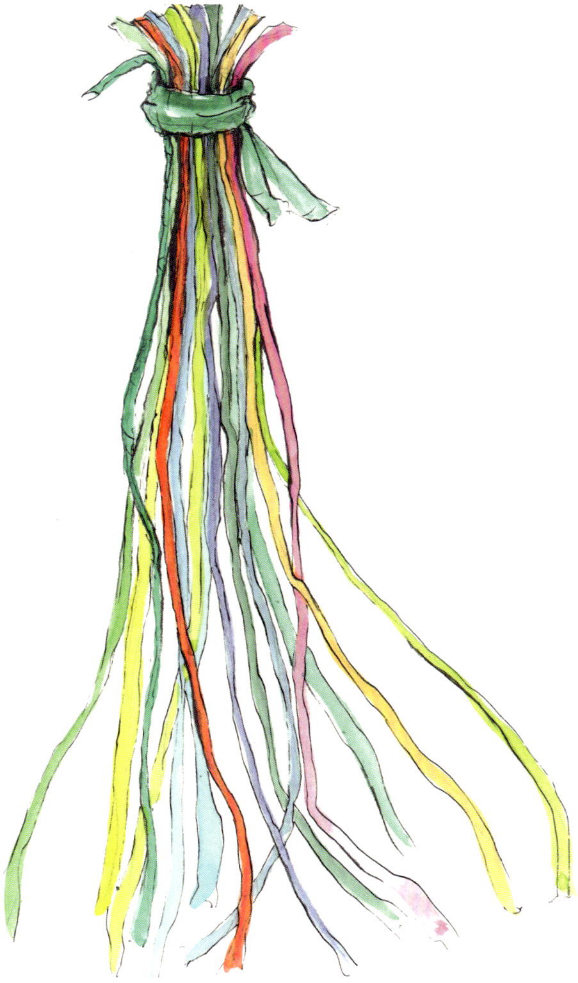

not a soul must know. Am I unfit to be the minister? It would never do to let on that I can't see the cloth."

"Don't hesitate to tell us what you think of it," said one of the weavers.

"Oh, it's beautiful - it's enchanting." The old minister peered through his spectacles. "Such a pattern, what colours!" I'll be sure to tell the Emperor how delighted I am with it."

"We're pleased to hear that," the swindlers said. They proceeded to name all the colours and to explain the intricate pattern. The old minister paid the closest attention, so that he could tell it all to the Emperor. And so he did.

The swindlers at once asked for more money, more silk and gold thread, to get on with the weaving. But it all went into their pockets. Not a thread went into the looms, though they worked at their weaving as hard as ever.

The Emperor presently sent another trustworthy official to see how the work progressed and how soon it would be ready. The same thing happened to him that had happened to the minister. He looked and he looked, but as there was nothing to see in the looms he couldn't see anything.

"Isn't it a beautiful piece of goods?" the swindlers asked him, as they displayed and described their imaginary pattern.

"I know I'm not stupid," the man thought, "so it must be that I'm unworthy of my good office. That's strange. I mustn't let anyone find it out, though." So he praised the material he did not see. He declared he was delighted with the beautiful colours and the exquisite pattern. To the Emperor he said, "It held me spellbound."

All the town was talking of this splendid cloth, and the Emperor wanted to see it for himself while it was still in the looms. Attended by a band of chosen men, among whom were his two old trusted officials - the ones who had been to the weavers - he set out to see the two swindlers. He found them weaving with might and main, but without a thread in their looms.

"Magnificent," said the two officials already duped. "Just look, Your Majesty, what colours! What a design!" They pointed to the empty looms, each supposing that the others could see the stuff.

"What's this?" thought the Emperor. "I can't see anything. This is terrible!

Am I a fool? Am I unfit to be the Emperor? What a thing to happen to me of all people! - Oh! It's very pretty," he said. "It has my highest approval." And he nodded approbation at the empty loom. Nothing could make him say that he couldn't see anything.

His whole retinue stared and stared. One saw no more than another, but they all joined the Emperor in exclaiming, "Oh! It's

very pretty," and they advised him to wear clothes made of this wonderful cloth especially for the great procession he was soon to lead. "Magnificent! Excellent! Unsurpassed!" were bandied from mouth to mouth, and everyone did his best to seem well pleased. The Emperor gave each of the swindlers a cross to wear in his buttonhole, and the title of "Sir Weaver."

Before the procession the swindlers sat up all night and burned more than six candles, to show how busy they were finishing the Emperor's new clothes. They pretended to take the cloth off the loom. They made cuts in the air with huge scissors. And at last they said, "Now the Emperor's new clothes are ready for him."

Then the Emperor himself came with his noblest noblemen, and the swindlers each raised an arm as if they were holding something. They said, "These are the trousers, here's the coat, and this is the mantle," naming each garment. "All of them are as light as a spider web. One would almost think he had nothing on, but that's what makes them so fine."

"Exactly," all the noblemen agreed, though they could see nothing, for there was nothing to see.

"If Your Imperial Majesty will condescend to take your clothes off," said the swindlers, "we will help you on with your new ones here in front of the long mirror." The Emperor undressed, and the swindlers pretended to put his new clothes on him, one garment after another. They took him around the waist and seemed to be fastening something - that was his train -as the Emperor turned round and round before the mirror.

"How well Your Majesty's new clothes look. Aren't they becoming!" He heard on all sides, "That pattern, so perfect! Those colours, so suitable! It is a magnificent outfit." Then the minister of public processions announced: "Your Majesty's canopy is waiting outside." "Well, I'm supposed to be ready," the Emperor said, and turned again for one last look in the mirror. "It is a remarkable fit, isn't it?" He seemed to regard his costume with the greatest interest.

The noblemen who were to carry his train stooped low and reached for the floor as if they were picking up his mantle. Then they pretended to lift and hold it high. They didn't dare admit they had nothing to hold.

So off went the Emperor in procession under his splendid canopy. Everyone in the streets and the windows said, "Oh, how fine are the Emperor's new clothes! Don't they fit him to perfection? And see his long train!" Nobody would confess that he couldn't see anything, for that would prove him either unfit for his position, or a fool. No costume the Emperor had worn before was ever such a complete success.

"But he hasn't got anything on," a little child said. "Did you ever hear such innocent prattle?" said its father. And one person whispered to another what the child had said, "He hasn't anything on. A child says he hasn't anything on."

"But he hasn't got anything on!" the whole town cried out at last.

The Emperor shivered, for he suspected they were right. But he thought, "This procession has got to go on." So he walked more proudly than ever, as his noblemen held high the train that wasn't there at all.

# The Princess and the Pea

Once upon a time, there was a Prince who wanted to marry a Princess. Only a real one would do. So he traveled through all the world to find her, and everywhere things went wrong. There were Princesses aplenty, but how was he to know whether they were real Princesses? There was something not quite right about them all. So he came home again and was unhappy, because he did so want to have a real Princess.

One evening a terrible storm blew up. It lightened and thundered and rained. It was really frightful! In the midst of it all came a knocking at the

town gate. The old King went to open it.

Who should be standing outside but a Princess, and what a sight she was in all that rain and wind. Water streamed from her hair down her clothes into her shoes, and ran out at the heels. Yet she claimed to be a real Princess.

"We'll soon find that out," the old Queen thought to herself. Without saying a word about it she went to the bedchamber, stripped back the bedclothes, and put just one pea in the bottom of the bed. Then she took twenty mattresses and piled them on the pea. Then she took twenty eiderdown feather beds and piled them on the mattresses.

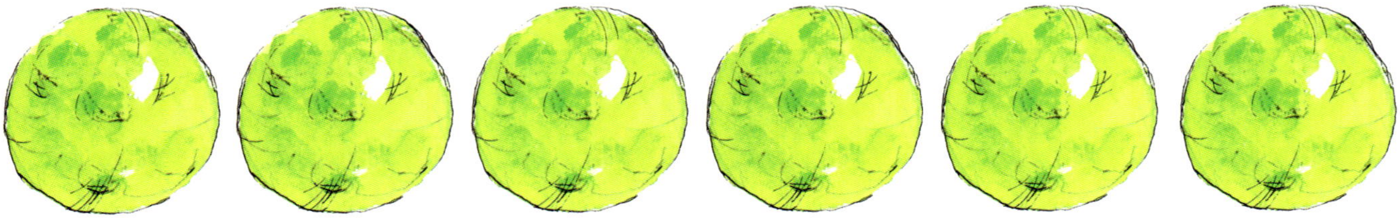

Up on top of all these the Princess was to spend the night.

In the morning they asked her, "Did you sleep well?"

" Oh!" said the Princess. "No. I scarcely slept at all. Heaven knows what's in that bed. I lay on something so hard that I'm black and blue all over. It was simply terrible."

They could see she was a real Princess and no question about it, now that she had felt one pea all the way through twenty mattresses and twenty more feather beds. Nobody but a Princess could be so delicate. So the Prince made haste to marry her, because he knew he had found a real Princess.

As for the pea, they put it in the museum. There it's still to be seen, unless somebody has taken it.

There, that's a true story.

# The Steadfast Tin Soldier

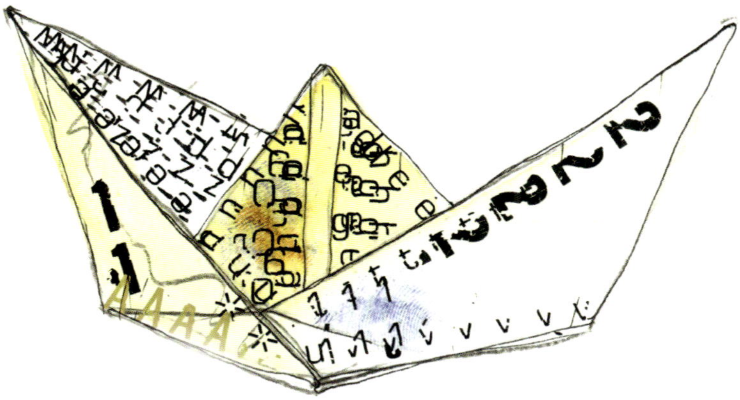

Once upon a time there were twenty-five tin soldiers. They were all brothers, born of the same old tin spoon. They shouldered their muskets and looked straight ahead of them, splendid in their uniforms, all red and blue.

The very first thing in the world that they heard was, "Tin soldiers!" A small boy shouted it and clapped his hands as the lid was lifted off their box on his birthday. He immediately set them up on the table.

All the soldiers looked exactly alike except one. He looked a little different as he had been cast last of all. The tin was short, so he had only one leg. But there he stood, as steady on one leg as any of the other soldiers on their two. But just you see, he'll be the remarkable one.

On the table with the soldiers were many other playthings, and one that no eye could miss was a marvelous castle of cardboard. It had little windows through which you could look right inside it. And in front of the castle were miniature trees around a little mirror supposed to represent a lake. The wax swans that swam on its surface were reflected in the mirror. All this was very pretty but prettiest of all was the little lady who stood in the open doorway of the castle. Though she was a paper doll, she wore a dress of the fluffiest gauze. A tiny blue ribbon went over her shoulder for a scarf, and in the middle of it shone a spangle that was as big as her face. The little lady held out both her arms, as a ballet dancer does, and one leg was lifted so high behind her that the tin soldier couldn't see it at all, and he supposed she must have only one leg, as he did.

"That would be a wife for me," he thought. "But maybe she's too grand. She lives in a castle. I have only a box, with four-and-twenty roommates to share it. That's no place for

her. But I must try to make her acquaintance." Still as stiff as when he stood at attention, he lay down on the table behind a snuffbox, where he could admire the dainty little dancer who kept standing on one leg without ever losing her balance.

When the evening came the other tin soldiers were put away in their box, and the people of the house went to bed. Now the toys began to play among themselves at visits, and battles, and at giving balls. The tin soldiers rattled about in their box, for they wanted to play too, but they could not get the lid open. The nutcracker turned somersaults, and the slate pencil squeaked out jokes on the slate. The toys made such a noise that they woke up the canary bird, who made them a speech, all in verse. The only two who stayed still were the tin soldier and the little dancer.

Without ever swerving from the tip of one toe, she held out her arms to him, and the tin soldier was just as steadfast on his one leg. Not once did he take his eyes off her.

Then the clock struck twelve and - clack! - up popped the lid of the

snuffbox. But there was no snuff in it, no - out bounced a little black bogey, a jack-in-the-box.

"Tin soldier," he said. "Will you please keep your eyes to yourself?" The tin soldier pretended not to hear.

The bogey said, "Just you wait till tomorrow."

But when morning came, and the children got up, the soldier was set on the window ledge. And whether the bogey did it, or there was a gust of wind, all of a sudden the window flew open and the soldier pitched out headlong from the third floor. He fell at breathtaking speed and landed cap first, with his bayonet buried between the paving stones and his one leg stuck straight in the air. The housemaid and the little boy ran down to look for him and, though they nearly stepped on the tin soldier, they walked right past without seeing him. If the soldier had called, "Here I am!" they would surely have found him, but he thought it contemptible to raise an uproar while he was wearing his uniform.

Soon it began to rain. The drops fell faster and faster, until they came down by the bucketful. As soon as the rain let up, along came two young rapscallions.

"Hi, look!" one of them said, "there's a tin soldier. Let's send him sailing."

They made a boat out of newspaper, put the tin soldier in the middle of it, and away he went down the gutter with the two young rapscallions running beside him and clapping their hands. High heavens! How the waves splashed, and how fast the water ran down the gutter. Don't forget that it had just been raining by the bucketful. The paper boat pitched, and tossed, and sometimes it whirled about so rapidly that it made the soldier's head spin. But he stood as steady as ever. Never once flinching, he kept his eyes front, and carried his gun shoulder-high. Suddenly the boat rushed under a long plank where the gutter was boarded over. It was as dark as the soldier's own box.

"Where can I be going?" the soldier wondered. "This must be that black bogey's revenge. Ah! if only I had the little lady with me, it could be

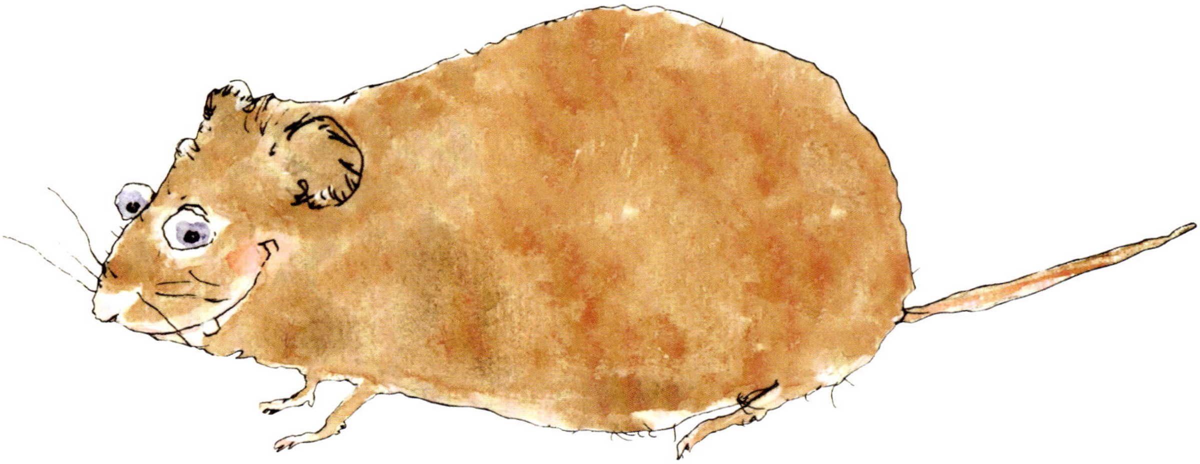

twice as dark here for all that I would care."

Out popped a great water rat who lived under the gutter plank.

"Have you a passport?" said the rat. "Hand it over."

The soldier kept quiet and held his musket tighter. On rushed the boat, and the rat came right after it, gnashing his teeth as he called to the sticks and straws:

"Halt him! Stop him! He didn't pay his toll. He hasn't shown his passport. "But the current ran stronger and stronger. The soldier could see daylight ahead where the board ended, but he also heard a roar that would frighten the bravest of us. Hold on! Right at the end of that gutter plank the water poured into the great canal. It was as dangerous to him as a waterfall would be to us.

He was so near it he could not possibly stop. The boat plunged into the whirlpool. The poor tin soldier stood as staunch as he could, and no one can say that he so much as blinked an eye. Thrice and again the boat spun around. It filled to the top - and was bound to sink. The water was up to his neck and still the boat went down, deeper, deeper, deeper, and the paper got soft and limp. Then the water rushed over his head. He thought of the pretty little dancer whom he'd never see again, and in his ears rang an old, old song:

"Farewell, farewell, O warrior brave, Nobody can from Death thee save."

And now the paper boat broke beneath him, and the soldier sank right through. And just at that moment he was swallowed by a most enormous fish.

My! how dark it was inside that fish. It was darker than under the gutter-plank and it was so cramped, but the tin soldier still was staunch. He lay there full length, soldier fashion, with musket to shoulder.

Then the fish flopped and floundered in a most unaccountable way. Finally it was perfectly still, and after a while something struck through him like a flash of lightning. The tin soldier saw daylight again, and he heard a voice say, "The Tin Soldier!" The fish had been caught, carried to market, bought, and brought to a kitchen where the cook cut him open with her big knife.

She picked the soldier up bodily between her two fingers, and carried him off upstairs. Everyone wanted to see this remarkable traveler who had traveled about in a fish's stomach, but the tin soldier took no pride in it. They put him on the table and-lo and behold, what curious things can happen in this world-there he was, back in the same room as before. He saw the same children, the same toys were on the table, and there was the same fine castle with the pretty little

dancer. She still balanced on one leg, with the other raised high. She too was steadfast. That touched the soldier so deeply that he would have cried tin tears, only soldiers never cry. He looked at her, and she looked at him, and never a word was said. Just as things were going so nicely for them, one of the little boys snatched up the tin soldier and threw him into the stove. He did it for no reason at all. That black bogey in the snuffbox must have put him up to it.

The tin soldier stood there dressed in flames. He felt a terrible heat, but whether it came from the flames or from his love he didn't know. He'd lost his splendid colours, maybe from his hard journey, maybe from grief, nobody can say.

He looked at the little lady, and she looked at him, and he felt himself melting. But still he stood steadfast, with his musket held trim on his shoulder.

Then the door blew open. A puff of wind struck the dancer. She flew like a sylph, straight into the fire with the soldier, blazed up in a flash, and was gone. The tin soldier melted, all in a lump. The next day, when a servant took up the ashes she found him in the shape of a little tin heart. But of the pretty dancer nothing was left except her spangle, and it was burned as black as a coal.

# The Ugly Duckling

It was so beautiful out on the country, it was summer- the wheat fields were golden, the oats were green, and down among the green meadows the hay was stacked. There the stork minced about on his red legs, clacking away in Egyptian, which was the language his mother had taught him. Round about the field and meadow lands rose vast forests, in which deep lakes lay hidden. Yes, it was indeed lovely out there in the country.

In the midst of the sunshine there stood an old manor house that had a deep moat around it. From the walls of the manor right down to the water's edge great burdock leaves grew, and there were some so tall that little children could stand upright beneath the biggest of them. In this wilderness of leaves, which was as dense as the forests itself, a duck sat on her nest, hatching her ducklings. She was becoming somewhat weary, because sitting is such a dull business and scarcely anyone came to see her. The other ducks would much rather swim in the moat than waddle out and squat under the burdock leaf to gossip with her.

But at last the eggshells began to crack, one after another. "Peep, peep!" said the little things, as they came to life and poked out their heads.

"Quack, quack!" said the duck, and quick as quick can be they all

waddled out to have a look at the green world under the leaves. Their mother let them look as much as they pleased, because green is good for the eyes. "How wide the world is," said all the young ducks, for they certainly had much more room now than they had when they were in their eggshells.

"Do you think this is the whole world?" their mother asked. "Why it extends on and on, clear across to the other side of the garden and right on into the parson's field, though that is further than I have ever been. I do hope you are all hatched," she said as she got up. "No, not quite all. The biggest egg still lies here. How much longer is this going to take? I am really rather tired of it all," she said, but she settled back on her nest.

"Well, how goes it?" asked an old duck who came to pay her a call.

"It takes a long time with that one egg," said the duck on the nest. "It won't crack, but look at the others. They are the cutest little ducklings I've ever seen. They look exactly like their father, the wretch! He hasn't come to see me at all."

"Let's have a look at the egg that won't crack," the old duck said. "It's a turkey egg, and you can take my word for it. I was fooled like that

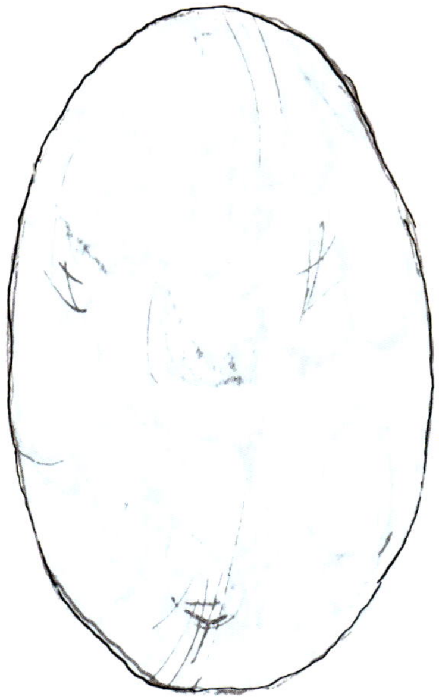

once myself. What trouble and care I had with those turkey children, for I may as well tell you, they are afraid of the water. I simply could not get them into it. I quacked and snapped at them, but it wasn't a bit of use. Let me see the egg. Certainly, it's a turkey egg. Let it lie, and go teach your other children to swim."

"Oh, I'll sit a little longer. I've been at it so long already that I may as well sit here half the summer."

"Suit yourself," said the old duck, and away she waddled.

At last the big egg did crack. "Peep," said the young one, and out he tumbled, but he was so big and ugly. The duck took a look at him. "That's a frightfully big duckling," she said. "He doesn't look the least like the others. Can he really be a turkey baby? Well, well! I'll soon find out. Into the water he shall go, even if I have to shove him in myself."

Next day the weather was perfectly splendid, and the sun shone down on all the green burdock leaves. The mother duck led her whole family down to the moat. Splash! she took to the water. "Quack, quack," said she, and one duckling after another plunged in. The water went over their heads, but they came up in a flash, and floated to perfection. Their legs worked automatically, and they were all there in the water. Even the big, ugly grey one was swimming along.

"Why, that's no turkey," she said. "See how nicely he uses his legs, and how straight he holds himself. He's my very own son after all, and quite good-looking if you look at him properly. Quack, quack come with me. I'll lead you out into the world and introduce you to the duck yard.

But keep close to me so that you won't get stepped on, and watch out for the cat!"

Thus they sallied into the duck yard, where all was in an uproar because two families were fighting over the head of an eel. But the cat got it, after all.

"You see, that's the way of the world." The mother duck licked her bill because she wanted the eel's head for herself. "Stir your legs. Bustle about, and mind that you bend your necks to that old duck over there. She's the noblest of us all, and has Spanish blood in her. That's why she's so fat. See that red rag around her leg? That's a wonderful thing, and the highest distinction a duck can get. It shows that they don't want to lose her, and that she's to have special attention from man and beast. Shake yourselves! Don't turn your toes in. A well-bred duckling turns his toes way out, just as his father and mother do-this way. So then! Now duck your necks and say quack!"

They did as she told them, but the other ducks around them looked on and said right out loud, "See here! Must we have this brood too, just as if there weren't enough of us already? And-fie! what an ugly-looking fellow that duckling is! We won't stand for him." One duck charged up and bit his neck.

"Let him alone," his mother said. "He isn't doing any harm."

"Possibly not," said the duck who bit him, "but he's too big and strange, and therefore he needs a good whacking."

"What nice-looking children you have, Mother," said the old duck with the rag around her leg. "They are all pretty except that one. He didn't come out so well. It's a pity you can't hatch him again." "That can't be

managed, your ladyship," said the mother. "He isn't so handsome, but he's as good as can be, and he swims just as well as the rest, or, I should say, even a little better than they do. I hope his looks will improve with age, and after a while he won't seem so big. He took too long in the egg, and that's why his figure isn't all that it should be." She pinched his neck and preened his feathers. "Moreover, he's a drake, so it won't matter so much. I think he will be quite strong, and I'm sure he will amount to something."

"The other ducklings are pretty enough," said the old duck. "Now make yourselves right at home, and if you find an eel's head you may bring it to me."

So they felt quite at home. But the poor duckling who had been the last one out of his egg, and who looked so ugly, was pecked and pushed about and made fun of by the ducks, and the chickens as well. “He’s too big,” said they all. The turkey gobbler, who thought himself an emperor because he was born wearing spurs, puffed up like a ship under full sail and bore down upon him, gobbling and gobbling until he was red in the face. The poor duckling did not know where he dared stand or where he dared walk. He was so sad because he was so desperately ugly, and because he was the laughing stock of the whole barnyard.

So it went on the first day, and after that things went from bad to worse. The poor duckling was chased and buffeted about by everyone. Even his own brothers and sisters abused him. “Oh,” they would always say, “how we wish the cat would catch you, you ugly thing.” And his mother said, “How I do wish you were miles away.” The ducks nipped him, and the hens pecked him, and the girl who fed them kicked him with her foot.

So he ran away; and he flew over the fence. The little birds in the bushes darted up in a fright. “That’s because I’m so ugly,” he thought, and closed his eyes, but he ran on just the same until he reached the great marsh where the wild ducks lived. There he lay all night long, weary and disheartened.

When morning came, the

wild ducks flew up to have a look at their new companion. "What sort of creature are you?" they asked, as the duckling turned in all directions, bowing his best to them all. "You are terribly ugly," they told him, "but that's nothing to us so long as you don't marry into our family."

Poor duckling! Marriage certainly had never entered his mind. All he wanted was for them to let him lie among the reeds and drink a little water from the marsh.

There he stayed for two whole days. Then he met two wild geese, or rather wild ganders-for they were males. They had not been out of the shell very long, and that's what made them so sure of themselves.

"Say there, comrade," they said, "you're so ugly that we have taken a fancy to you. Come with us and be a bird of passage. In another marsh nearby, there are some fetching wild geese, all nice young ladies who know how to quack. You are so ugly that you'll completely turn their heads."

Bing! Bang! Shots rang in the air, and these two ganders fell dead among the reeds. The water was red with their blood. Bing! Bang! the shots rang, and as whole flocks of wild geese flew up from the reeds another volley crashed. A great hunt was in progress. The hunters lay under cover all around the marsh, and some even perched on branches of trees that overhung the reeds. Blue smoke rose like clouds from the shade of the trees, and drifted far out over the water.

The bird dogs came splash, splash! through the swamp, bending down the reeds and the rushes on every side. This gave the poor duckling such a fright that he twisted his head about to hide it under his wing. But at that very moment a fearfully big dog appeared right beside him. His tongue lolled out of his mouth and his wicked eyes glared horribly. He opened his wide jaws, flashed his sharp teeth, and - splash, splash - on he went without touching the duckling.

"Thank heavens," he sighed, "I'm so ugly that the dog won't even bother to bite me."

He lay perfectly still, while the bullets splattered through the reeds as shot after shot was fired. It was late in the day before things became quiet again, and even then the poor duckling didn't dare move. He waited several hours before he ventured to look about him, and then he scurried away from that marsh as fast as he could go. He ran across field and meadows. The wind was so strong that he had to struggle to keep his feet.

Late in the evening he came to a miserable little hovel, so ramshackle that it did not know which way to tumble, and that was the only reason it still stood. The wind struck the duckling so hard that the poor little fellow had to sit down on his tail to withstand it. The storm blew stronger and stronger, but the duckling noticed that one hinge had come loose and the door hung so crooked that he could squeeze through the

crack into the room, and that's just what he did.

Here lived an old woman with her cat and her hen. The cat, whom she called "Sonny," could arch his back, purr, and even make sparks, though for that you had to stroke his fur the wrong way. The hen had short little legs, so she was called "Chickey Shortleg." She laid good eggs, and the old woman loved her as if she had been her own child.

In the morning they were quick to notice the strange duckling. The cat began to purr, and the hen began to cluck.

"What on earth!" The old woman looked around, but she was short-sighted, and she mistook the duckling for a fat duck that had lost its way.

"That was a good catch," she said. "Now I shall have duck eggs-unless it's a drake. We must try it out." So the duckling was tried out for three weeks, but not one egg did he lay.

In this house the cat was master and the hen was mistress. They always said, "We and the world," for they thought themselves half of the world, and much the better half at that. The duckling thought that there might be more than one way of thinking, but the hen would not hear of it.

"Can you lay eggs?" she asked

"No."

"Then be so good as to hold your tongue."

The cat asked, "Can you arch your back, purr, or make sparks?"

"No."

"Then keep your opinion to yourself when sensible people are talking."

The duckling sat in a corner, feeling most despondent. Then he remembered the fresh air and the sunlight. Such a desire to go swimming on the water possessed him that he could not help telling the hen about it.

"What on earth has come over you?" the hen cried. "You haven't a thing to do, and that's why you get such silly notions. Lay us an egg, or learn to purr, and you'll get over it."

"But it's so refreshing to float on the water," said the duckling, "so refreshing to feel it rise over your head as you dive to the bottom."

"Yes, it must be a great pleasure!" said the hen. "I think you must have gone crazy. Ask the cat, who's the wisest fellow I know, whether he likes to swim or dive down in the water. Of myself I say nothing. But ask the old woman, our mistress. There's no one on earth wiser than she is. Do you imagine she wants to go swimming and feel the water rise over her head?"

"You don't understand me," said the duckling.

"Well, if we don't, who would? Surely you don't think you are cleverer than the cat and the old woman - to say nothing of myself. Don't be so conceited, child. Just thank your Maker for all the kindness we have shown you. Didn't you get into this snug room, and fall in with people who can tell you what's what? But you are such a numbskull that it's no pleasure to have you around.

Believe me, I tell you this for your own good. I say unpleasant truths, but that's the only way you can know who are your friends. Be sure now that you lay some eggs. See to it that you learn to purr or to make sparks."

"I think I'd better go out into the wide world," said the duckling.

"Suit yourself," said the hen.

So off went the duckling. He swam on the water, and dived down in it, but still he was slighted by every living creature because of his ugliness.

Autumn came on. The leaves in the forest turned yellow and brown.

The wind took them and whirled them about. The heavens looked cold as the low clouds hung heavy with snow and hail. Perched on the fence, the raven screamed, “Caw, caw!” and trembled with cold. It made one shiver to think of it. Pity the poor little duckling!

One evening, just as the sun was setting in splendour, a great flock of large, handsome birds appeared out of the reeds. The duckling had never seen birds so beautiful. They were dazzling white, with long graceful necks. They were swans. They uttered a very strange cry as they unfurled their magnificent wings to fly from this cold land, away to warmer countries and to open waters. They went up so high, so very high, that the ugly little duckling felt a strange uneasiness come over him as he watched them. He went around and round in the water, like a wheel. He craned his neck to follow their course, and gave a cry so shrill and strange that he frightened himself. Oh! He could not forget them-those splendid, happy birds. When he could no longer see them he dived to the very bottom. and when he came up again he was quite beside himself. He did not know what birds they were or whither they were bound, yet he loved them more than anything he had ever loved before. It was not that he envied them, for how could he ever dare dream of wanting their marvelous beauty for himself? He would have been

grateful if only the ducks would have tolerated him-the poor ugly creature.

The winter grew cold - so bitterly cold that the duckling had to swim to and fro in the water to keep it from freezing over. But every night the hole in which he swam kept getting smaller and smaller. Then it froze so hard that the duckling had to paddle continuously to keep the crackling ice from closing in upon him. At last, too tired to move, he was frozen fast in the ice.

Early that morning a farmer came by, and when he saw how things were he went out on the pond, broke away the ice with his wooden shoe, and carried the duckling home to his wife. There the duckling revived, but when the children wished to play with him he thought they meant to hurt him. Terrified, he fluttered into the milk pail, splashing the whole room with milk. The woman shrieked and threw up her hands as he flew into the butter tub, and then in and out of the meal barrel. Imagine what he looked like now! The woman screamed and lashed out at him with the fire tongs. The children tumbled over each other as they tried to catch him, and they laughed and they shouted. Luckily the door was open, and the duckling escaped through it into the bushes, where he lay down, in the newly fallen snow, as if in a daze.

But it would be too sad to tell of all the hardships and wretchedness he had to endure during this cruel winter. When the warm sun shone once more, the duckling was still alive among the reeds of the marsh. The larks began to sing again. It was beautiful springtime.

Then, quite suddenly, he lifted his wings. They swept through the air much more strongly than before, and their powerful strokes carried him far. Before he quite knew what was happening, he found himself in a great garden where apple trees bloomed. The lilacs filled the air with sweet scent and hung in clusters from long, green branches that bent over a winding stream. Oh, but it was lovely here in the freshness of spring!

From the thicket before him came three lovely white swans. They ruffled their feathers and swam lightly in the stream. The duckling recognised these noble creatures, and a strange feeling of sadness came upon him.

"I shall fly near these royal birds, and they will peck me to bits because

I, who am so very ugly, dare to go near them. But I don't care. Better be killed by them than to be nipped by the ducks, pecked by the hens, kicked about by the hen-yard girl, or suffer such misery in winter."

So he flew into the water and swam toward the splendid swans. They saw him, and swept down upon him with their rustling feathers raised. "Kill me!" said the poor creature, and he bowed his head down over the water to wait for death. But what did he see there, mirrored in the clear stream? He beheld his own image, and it was no longer the reflection of a clumsy, dirty, gray bird, ugly and offensive. He himself was a swan! Being born in a duck yard does not matter, if only you are hatched from a swan's egg.

He felt quite glad that he had come through so much trouble and misfortune, for now he had a fuller understanding of his own good fortune, and of beauty when he met with it. The great swans swam all around him and stroked him with their bills.

Several little children came into the garden to throw grain and bits of bread upon the water. The smallest child cried, "Here's a new one," and the others rejoiced, "yes, a new one has come." They clapped their hands, danced around, and ran to bring their father and mother.

And they threw bread and cake upon the water, while they all agreed, "The new one is the most handsome of all. He's so young and so good-looking." The old swans bowed in his honour.

Then he felt very bashful, and tucked his head under his wing. He did not know what this was all about.

He felt so very happy, but he wasn't at all proud, for a good heart never grows proud. He thought about how he had been persecuted and scorned, and now he heard them all call him the most beautiful of all beautiful birds. The lilacs dipped their clusters into the stream before him, and the sun shone so warm and so heartening. He rustled his feathers and held his slender neck high, as he cried out with full heart: "I never dreamed there could be so much happiness, when I was the ugly duckling."

# The Little Mermaid

Far out in the ocean the water is as blue as the petals of the loveliest cornflower, and as clear as the purest glass. But it is very deep too. It goes down deeper than any anchor rope will go, and many, many steeples would have to be stacked one on top of another to reach from the bottom to the surface of the sea. It is down there that the sea folk live.

Now don't suppose that there are only bare white sands at the bottom of the sea. No indeed! The most marvelous trees and flowers grow down there, with such pliant stalks and leaves that the least stir in the water makes them move about as though they were alive. All sorts of fish, large and small, dart among the branches, just as birds flit through the

trees up here. From the deepest spot in the ocean rises the palace of the sea king. Its walls are made of coral and its high pointed windows of the clearest amber, but the roof is made of mussel shells that open and shut with the tide. This is a wonderful sight to see, for every shell holds glistening pearls, any one of which would be the pride of a queen's crown.

The sea king down there had been a widower for years, and his old mother kept house for him. She was a clever woman, but very proud of her noble birth. Therefore she flaunted twelve oysters on her tail while the other ladies of the court were only allowed to wear six. Except for this she was an altogether praiseworthy person, particularly so because she was extremely fond of her granddaughters, the little sea princesses. They were six lovely girls, but the youngest was the most beautiful of them all. Her skin was as soft and tender as a rose petal, and her eyes were as blue as the deep sea, but like all the others she had no feet. Her body ended in a fish tail.

The whole day long they used to play in the palace, down in the great halls where live flowers grew on the walls. Whenever the high amber windows were thrown open the fish would swim in, just as swallows dart into our rooms when we open the windows. But these fish, now, would swim right up to the little princesses to eat out of their hands and let themselves be petted.

Outside the palace was a big garden, with flaming red and deep-blue trees. Their fruit glittered like gold, and their blossoms flamed like fire on their constantly waving stalks. The soil was very fine sand indeed, but as blue as burning brimstone. A strange blue veil lay over everything down there. You would have thought yourself aloft in the air with only the blue sky above and beneath you, rather than down at the bottom of the sea. When there was a dead calm, you could just see the sun, like a scarlet flower with light streaming from its calyx.

Each little princess had her own small garden plot, where she could dig and plant whatever she liked. One of them made her little flower bed in the shape of a whale, another thought it neater to shape hers like a little mermaid, but the youngest of them made hers as round as the sun, and there she grew only flowers which were as red as the sun itself. She was an unusual child, quiet and wistful, and when her sisters decorated their gardens with all kinds of odd things they had found in sunken ships, she would allow nothing in hers except flowers as red as the sun, and a pretty marble statue. This figure of a handsome boy, carved in pure white marble, had sunk down to the bottom of the sea from some ship that was wrecked. Beside the statue she planted a rose-coloured weeping willow tree, which thrived so well that its graceful branches shaded the statue and hung down to the blue sand, where their shadows took on a violet tint, and swayed as the branches swayed. It looked as if the roots and the tips of the branches were kissing each other in play.

Nothing gave the youngest princess such pleasure as to hear about the world of human beings up above them. Her old grandmother had to tell her all she knew about ships and cities, and of people and animals. What seemed nicest of all to her was that up on land the flowers were fragrant, for those at the bottom of the sea had no scent. And she thought it was nice that the woods

were green, and that the fish you saw among their branches could sing so loud and sweet that it was delightful to hear them. Her grandmother had to call the little birds "fish," or the princess would not have known what she was talking about, for she had never seen a bird.

"When you get to be fifteen," her grandmother said, "you will be allowed to rise up out of the ocean and sit on the rocks in the moonlight, to watch the great ships sailing by. You will see woods and towns, too."

Next year one of her sisters would be fifteen, but the others - well, since each was a whole year older than the next the youngest still had five long years to wait until she could rise up from the water and see what our world was like. But each sister promised to tell the others about all that she saw, and what she found most marvelous on her first day. Their grandmother had not told them half enough, and there were so many thing that they longed to know about.

The most eager of them all was the youngest, the very one who was

so quiet and wistful. Many a night she stood by her open window and looked up through the dark blue water where the fish waved their fins and tails. She could just see the moon and stars. To be sure, their light was quite dim, but looked at through the water they seemed much bigger than they appear to us. Whenever a cloud-like shadow swept across them, she knew that it was either a whale swimming overhead, or a ship with many human beings aboard it. Little did they dream that a pretty young mermaid was down below, stretching her white arms up toward the keel of their ship.

The eldest princess had her fifteenth birthday, so now she received permission to rise up out of the water. When she got back she had a hundred things to tell her sisters about, but the most marvelous thing of all, she said, was to lie on a sand bar in the moonlight, when the sea was calm, and to gaze at the large city on the shore, where the lights twinkled like hundreds of stars; to

listen to music; to hear the chatter and clamour of carriages and people; to see so many church towers and spires; and to hear the ringing bells. Because she could not enter the city, that was just what she most dearly longed to do.

Oh, how intently the youngest sister listened. After this, whenever she stood at her open window at night and looked up through the dark blue waters, she thought of that great city with all of its clatter and clamour, and even fancied that in these depths she could hear the church bells ring. The next year,

her second sister had permission to rise up to the surface and swim wherever she pleased. She came up just at sunset, and she said that this spectacle was the most marvelous sight she had ever seen. The heavens had a golden glow, and as for the clouds - she could not find words to describe their beauty. Splashed with red and tinted with violet, they sailed over her head. But much faster than the sailing clouds were wild swans in a flock. Like a long white veil trailing above the sea, they flew toward the setting sun. She too swam toward it, but down it went, and all the rose-coloured glow faded from the sea and sky. The following year, her third sister ascended, and as she was the boldest of them all she swam up a broad river that flowed into the ocean. She saw gloriously green, vine-colored hills. Palaces and manor houses could be glimpsed through the splendid woods. She heard all the birds sing, and the sun shone so brightly that often she had to dive under the water to cool her burning face. In a small cove she found a whole school of mortal children, paddling about in the water quite naked. She wanted to play with them, but they took fright and ran away. Then along came a little black animal - it was a dog, but she had never seen a dog before. It barked at her so ferociously that she took fright herself, and fled to the open sea. But never could she forget the splendid woods, the green hills, and the nice children who could swim in the water although they didn't wear fish tails.

The fourth sister was not so venturesome. She stayed far out among the rough waves, which she said was a marvelous place. You could see all around you for miles and miles, and the heavens up above you were like a vast dome of glass. She had seen ships, but they were so far away that they looked like sea gulls. Playful dolphins had turned somersaults, and monstrous whales had spouted water through their nostrils so that it looked as if hundreds of fountains were playing all around them.

Now the fifth sister had her turn. Her birthday came in the wintertime, so she saw things that none of the others had seen. The sea was a deep green color, and enormous icebergs drifted about. Each one glistened like a pearl, she said, but they were more lofty than any church steeple built by man. They assumed the most fantastic shapes, and sparkled like diamonds. She had seated herself on the largest one, and all the ships that came sailing by sped away as soon as the frightened sailors saw her there with her long hair blowing in the wind.

In the late evening clouds filled the sky. Thunder cracked and lightning darted across the heavens. Black waves lifted those great bergs of ice on high, where they flashed when the lightning struck.

On all the ships the sails were reefed and there was fear and trembling. But quietly she sat there, upon her drifting iceberg, and watched the blue forked lightning strike the sea.

Each of the sisters took delight in the lovely new sights when she first

rose up to the surface of the sea. But when they became grown-up girls, who were allowed to go wherever they liked, they became indifferent to it. They would become homesick, and in a month they said that there was no place like the bottom of the sea, where they felt so completely at home.

On many an evening the older sisters would rise to the surface, arm in arm, all five in a row. They had beautiful voices, more charming than those of any mortal beings. When a storm was brewing, and they anticipated a shipwreck, they would swim before the ship and sing most seductively of how beautiful it was at the bottom of the ocean, trying to overcome the prejudice that the sailors had against coming down to them. But people could not understand their song, and mistook it for the voice of the storm. Nor was it for them to see the glories of the deep. When their ship went down they were drowned, and it was as dead men that they reached the sea king's palace.

On the evenings when the mermaids rose through the water like this, arm in arm, their youngest sister stayed behind all alone, looking after them and wanting to weep. But a mermaid has no tears, and therefore she suffers so much more.

"Oh, how I do wish I were fifteen!" she said. "I know I shall love that world up there and all the people who live in it."

And at last she too came to be fifteen.

"Now I'll have you off my hands," said her grandmother, the old queen dowager. "Come, let me adorn you like your sisters." In the little maid's hair she put a wreath of white lilies, each petal of which was formed from half of a pearl. And the old queen let eight big oysters fasten themselves to the princess's tail, as a sign of her high rank.

"But that hurts!" said the little mermaid.

"You must put up with a good deal to keep up appearances," her grandmother told her.

Oh, how gladly she would have shaken off all these decorations, and laid aside the cumbersome wreath! The red flowers in her garden were much more becoming to her, but she didn't dare to make any changes. "Good-by," she said, and up she went through the water, as light and as sparkling as a bubble.

The sun had just gone down when her head rose above the surface, but the clouds still shone like gold and roses, and in the delicately tinted sky sparkled the clear gleam of the evening star. The air was mild and fresh and the sea unruffled. A great three-master lay in view with only one of all its sails set, for there was not even the whisper of a breeze, and the sailors idled about in the rigging and on the yards. There was music and singing on the ship, and as night came on they lighted hundreds of such brightly coloured lanterns that one might have thought the flags of all nations were swinging in the air.

The little mermaid swam right up

to the window of the main cabin, and each time she rose with the swell she could peep in through the clear glass panes at the crowd of brilliantly dressed people within. The handsomest of them all was a young Prince with big dark eyes. He could not be more than sixteen years old. It was his birthday and that was the reason for all the celebration. Up on deck the sailors were dancing, and when the Prince appeared among them a hundred or more rockets flew through the air, making it as bright as day. These startled the little mermaid so badly that she ducked under the water. But she soon peeped up again, and then it seemed as if all the stars in the sky were falling around her. Never had she seen such fireworks. Great suns spun around, splendid fire-fish floated through the blue air, and all these things were mirrored in the crystal clear sea. It was so brilliantly bright that you could see every little rope of the ship, and the people could be seen distinctly. Oh, how handsome the young Prince was! He laughed, and he smiled and shook people by the hand, while the music rang out in the perfect evening.

It got very late, but the little mermaid could not take her eyes off the ship and the handsome Prince. The brightly coloured lanterns were put out, no more rockets flew through the air, and no more cannon boomed. But there was a mutter and rumble deep down in the sea, and the swell kept bouncing her up so high that she could look into the cabin.

Now the ship began to sail. Canvas after canvas was spread in the wind, the waves rose high, great clouds gathered, and lightning flashed in the distance. Ah, they were in for a terrible storm, and the mariners made haste to reef the sails. The tall ship pitched and rolled as it sped through the angry sea. The waves rose up like towering black mountains, as if they would break over the masthead, but the swan - like ship plunged into the valleys between such waves, and emerged to ride their lofty heights. To the little mermaid this seemed good sport, but to the sailors it was nothing of the sort. The ship creaked and laboured, thick timbers gave way under the heavy blows, waves broke over the ship, the mainmast snapped in two like a reed, the ship listed over on its side, and water burst into the hold.

Now the little mermaid saw that people were in peril, and that she herself must take care to avoid the beams and wreckage tossed about by the sea. One moment it would be black as pitch, and she couldn't see a thing. Next moment the lightning would flash so brightly that she could distinguish every soul on board. Everyone was looking out for himself as best he could. She watched closely for the young Prince, and when the ship split in two she saw him sink down in the sea. At first she was overjoyed that he would be with her, but then she recalled that human people could not live under the water, and he could only visit her father's palace as a dead man. No, he should not die! So she swam in among all the floating planks and beams, completely forgetting that they might crush her. She dived through the waves and rode their crests, until at length she reached the young Prince, who was no longer able to swim in that raging sea. His arms and legs were exhausted, his beautiful eyes were closing, and he would have died if the little mermaid had not come to help him. She held his

head above water, and let the waves take them wherever the waves went.

At daybreak, when the storm was over, not a trace of the ship was in view. The sun rose out of the waters, red and bright, and its beams seemed to bring the glow of life back to the cheeks of the Prince, but his eyes remained closed. The mermaid kissed his high and shapely forehead. As she stroked his wet hair in place, it seemed to her that he looked like that marble statue in her little garden. She kissed him again and hoped that he would live.

She saw dry land rise before her in high blue mountains, topped with snow as glistening white as if a flock of swans were resting there. Down by the shore were splendid green woods, and in the foreground stood a church, or perhaps a convent; she didn't know which, but anyway it was a building. Orange and lemon trees grew in its garden, and tall palm trees grew beside the gateway. Here

the sea formed a little harbour, quite calm and very deep. Fine white sand had been washed up below the cliffs. She swam there with the handsome Prince, and stretched him out on the sand, taking special care to pillow his head up high in the warm sunlight.

The bells began to ring in the great white building, and a number of young girls came out into the garden. The little mermaid swam away behind some tall rocks that stuck out of the water. She covered her hair and her shoulders with foam so that no one could see her tiny face, and then she watched to see who would find the poor Prince.

In a little while one of the young girls came upon him. She seemed frightened, but only for a minute; then she called more people. The mermaid watched the Prince regain consciousness, and smile at everyone around him. But he did not smile at her, for he did not even know that she had saved him. She felt very unhappy, and when they led him away to the big building she dived sadly down into the water and returned to her father's palace.

She had always been quiet and wistful, and now she became much more so. Her sisters asked her what she had seen on her first visit up to the surface, but she would not tell them a thing. Many evenings and many mornings she revisited the spot where she had left the Prince. She saw the fruit in the garden ripened and harvested, and she saw the snow on the high mountain melted away, but she did not see the Prince, so each time she came home sadder than she had left. It was her one consolation to sit in her little garden and throw her arms about the beautiful marble

statue that looked so much like the Prince. But she took no care of her flowers now. They overgrew the paths until the place was a wilderness, and their long stalks and leaves became so entangled in the branches of the tree that it cast a gloomy shade.

Finally she couldn't bear it any longer. She told her secret to one of her sisters. Immediately all the other sisters heard about it. No one else knew, except a few more mermaids who told no one - except their most intimate friends. One of these friends knew who the Prince was. She too had seen the birthday celebration on the ship. She knew where he came from and where his kingdom was.

"Come, little sister!" said the other princesses. Arm in arm, they rose from the water in a long row, right in front of where they knew the Prince's palace stood. It was built of pale, glistening, golden stone with

great marble staircases, one of which led down to the sea. Magnificent gilt domes rose above the roof, and between the pillars all around the building were marble statues that looked most lifelike. Through the clear glass of the lofty windows one could see into the splendid halls, with their costly silk hangings and tapestries, and walls covered with paintings that were delightful to behold. In the center of the main hall a large fountain played its columns of spray up to the glass-domed roof, through which the sun shone down on the water and upon the lovely plants that grew in the big basin.

Now that she knew where he lived, many an evening and many a night she spent there in the sea. She swam much closer to shore than any of her sisters would dare venture, and she even went far up a narrow stream, under the splendid marble balcony that cast its long shadow in the water. Here she used to sit and watch the young Prince when he thought himself quite alone in the bright moonlight.

On many evenings she saw him sail out in his fine boat, with music playing and flags a-flutter. She would peep out through the green rushes, and if the wind blew her long silver veil, anyone who saw it mistook it for a swan spreading its wings.

On many nights she saw the fishermen come out to sea with their torches, and heard them tell about how kind the young Prince was. This made her proud to think that it was she who had saved his life when he was buffeted about, half dead among the waves. And she thought of how softly his head had rested on her breast, and how tenderly she had kissed him, though he knew nothing of all this nor could he even dream of it.

Increasingly she grew to like human beings, and more and more she longed to live among them. Their world seemed so much wider than her own, for they could skim over the sea in ships, and mount up into the lofty peaks high over the clouds, and their lands stretched out in woods and fields farther than the eye could see. There was so much she wanted to know. Her sisters could not answer all her questions, so she asked her old grandmother, who knew about the "upper world," which was what she said was the right name for the countries above the sea.

"If men aren't drowned," the little mermaid asked, "do they live on forever? Don't they die, as we do down here in the sea?"

"Yes," the old lady said, "they too must die, and their lifetimes are even shorter than ours. We can live to be three hundred years old, but when we perish we turn into mere foam on the sea, and haven't even a grave down here among our dear ones. We have no immortal soul, no life hereafter. We are like the green seaweed - once cut down, it never grows again. Human beings, on the contrary, have a soul which lives forever, long after their bodies have turned to clay. It rises through thin air, up to the shining stars. Just as we rise through the water to see the lands on earth, so men rise up to beautiful places unknown, which we shall never see."

"Why weren't we given an immortal soul?" the little mermaid

sadly asked. "I would gladly give up my three hundred years if I could be a human being only for a day, and later share in that heavenly realm."

"You must not think about that," said the old lady. "We fare much more happily and are much better off than the folk up there."

"Then I must also die and float as foam upon the sea, not hearing the music of the waves, and seeing neither the beautiful flowers nor the red sun! Can't I do anything at all to win an immortal soul?"

"No," her grandmother answered, "not unless a human being loved you so much that you meant more to him than his father and mother. If his every thought and his whole heart cleaved to you so that he would let a priest join his right hand to yours and would promise to be faithful here and throughout all eternity, then his soul would dwell in your body, and you would share in the happiness of mankind. He would give you a soul and yet keep his own. But that can never come to pass. The very thing that is your greatest beauty here in the sea - your fish tail - would be considered ugly on land. They have such poor taste that to be thought beautiful there you have to have two awkward props which they call legs."

The little mermaid sighed and looked unhappily at her fish tail.

"Come, let us be gay!" the old lady said. "Let us leap and bound throughout the three hundred years that we have to live. Surely that is time and to spare, and afterwards we shall be glad enough to rest in our graves. We are holding a court ball this evening."

This was a much more glorious affair than is ever to be seen on earth. The walls and the ceiling of the great ballroom were made of massive but transparent glass. Many hundreds of huge rose-red and grass-green shells stood on each side in rows, with the blue flames that burned in each shell illuminating the whole room and shining through the walls so clearly that it was quite bright in the sea outside. You could see the countless fish, great and small, swimming toward the glass walls. On some of them the scales gleamed purplish-red, while others were silver and gold. Across the floor of the hall ran a wide stream of water, and upon this the mermaids and mermen danced to their own entrancing songs. Such beautiful voices are not to be heard among the people who live on land. The little mermaid sang more sweetly than anyone else, and everyone applauded her. For a moment her heart was happy, because she knew she had the loveliest voice of all, in the sea or on the land. But her thoughts soon strayed to the world up above. She could not forget the charming Prince, nor her sorrow that she did not have an immortal soul like his. Therefore she stole out of her father's palace and, while everything there was song and gladness, she sat sadly in her own little garden.

Then she heard a bugle call through the water, and she thought, "That must mean he is sailing up there, he whom I love more than my father or mother, he of whom

I am always thinking, and in whose hands I would so willingly trust my lifelong happiness. I dare do anything to win him and to gain an immortal soul. While my sisters are dancing here, in my father's palace, I shall visit the sea witch of whom I have always been so afraid. Perhaps she will be able to advise me and help me."

The little mermaid set out from her garden toward the whirlpools that raged in front of the witch's dwelling. She had never gone that way before. No flowers grew there, nor any seaweed. Bare and gray, the sands extended to the whirlpools, where like roaring mill wheels the waters whirled and snatched everything within their reach down to the bottom of the sea. Between these tumultuous whirlpools she had to thread her way to reach the witch's waters, and then for a long stretch the only trail lay through a hot seething mire, which the witch called her peat marsh. Beyond it her house lay in the middle of a weird forest, where all the trees and shrubs were polyps, half animal and half plant. They looked like hundred-headed snakes growing out of the soil. All their branches were long, slimy arms, with fingers like wriggling worms. They squirmed, joint by joint, from their roots to their outermost tentacles, and whatever they could lay hold of they twined around and never let go. The little mermaid was terrified, and stopped at the edge of

the forest. Her heart thumped with fear and she nearly turned back, but then she remembered the Prince and the souls that men have, and she summoned her courage. She bound her long flowing locks closely about her head so that the polyps could not catch hold of them, folded her arms across her breast, and darted through the water like a fish, in among the slimy polyps that stretched out their writhing arms and fingers to seize her. She saw that every one of them held something that it had caught with its hundreds of little tentacles, and to which it clung as with strong hoops of steel. The white bones of men who had perished at sea and sunk to these depths could be seen in the polyps' arms. Ships' rudders, and seamen's

chests and treasures, and the skeletons of land animals had also fallen into their clutches, but the most ghastly sight of all was a little mermaid whom they had caught and strangled. She reached a large muddy clearing in the forest, where big fat water snakes slithered about, showing their foul yellowish bellies. In the middle of this clearing was a house built of the bones of shipwrecked men, and there sat the sea witch, letting a toad eat out of her mouth just as we might feed sugar to a little canary bird. She called the ugly fat water snakes her little chickabiddies, and let them crawl and sprawl about on her spongy bosom.

"I know exactly what you want," said the sea witch. "It is very foolish of you, but just the same you shall have your way, for it will bring you to grief, my proud princess. You want to get rid of your fish tail and have two props instead, so that you can walk about like a human creature, and have the young Prince fall in love with you, and win him and an immortal soul besides." At this, the witch gave such a loud cackling laugh that the toad and the snakes were shaken to the ground, where they lay writhing.

"You are just in time," said the witch. "After the sun comes up tomorrow, a whole year would have to go by before I could be of any help to you. I shall compound you a draught, and before sunrise you must swim to the shore with it, seat yourself on dry land, and drink the draught down. Then your tail will divide and shrink until it becomes what the people on earth call a pair of shapely legs. But it will hurt; it will feel as if a sharp sword slashed through you. Everyone who sees you will say that you are the most graceful human being they have ever laid eyes on, for you will keep your gliding movement and no dancer will be able to tread as lightly as you. But every step you take will feel as if you were treading upon knife blades so sharp that blood must flow. I am willing to help you, but are you willing to suffer all this?" "Yes," the little mermaid said in a trembling voice, as she thought of the Prince and of gaining a human soul.

"Remember!" said the witch. "Once you have taken a human form, you can

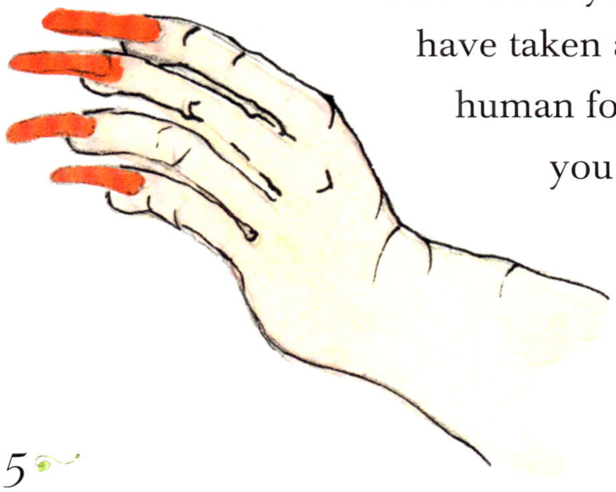

never be a mermaid again. You can never come back through the waters to your sisters, or to your father's palace. And if you do not win the love of the Prince so completely that for your sake he forgets his father and mother, cleaves to you with his every thought and his whole heart, and lets the priest join your hands in marriage, then you will win no immortal soul. If he marries someone else, your heart will break on the very next morning, and you will become foam of the sea."

"I shall take that risk," said the little mermaid, but she turned as pale as death.

"Also, you will have to pay me," said the witch, "and it is no trifling price that I'm asking. You have the sweetest voice of anyone down here at the bottom of the sea, and while I don't doubt that you would like to captivate the Prince with it, you must give this voice to me. I will take

the very best thing that you have, in return for my sovereign draught. I must pour my own blood in it to make the drink as sharp as a two-edged sword." "But if you take my voice," said the little mermaid, "what will be left to me?"

"Your lovely form," the witch told her, "your gliding movements, and your eloquent eyes. With these you can easily enchant a human heart. Well, have you lost your courage? Stick out your little tongue and I shall cut it off. I'll have my price, and you shall have the potent draught."

"Go ahead," said the little mermaid.

The witch hung her caldron over the flames, to brew the draught. "Cleanliness is a good thing," she said, as she tied her snakes in a knot and scoured out the pot with them. Then she pricked herself in the chest and let her black blood splash into the caldron. Steam swirled up from it, in such ghastly shapes that anyone would have been terrified by them. The witch constantly threw new ingredients into the caldron, and it started to boil with a sound like that of a crocodile shedding tears. When the draught was ready at last, it looked as clear as the purest water.

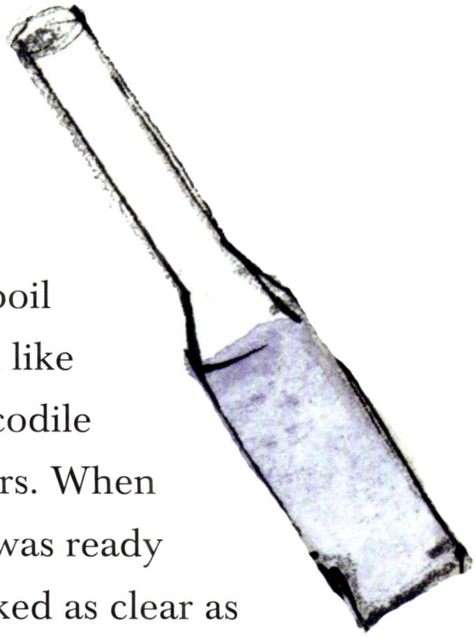

"There's your draught," said the witch. And she cut off the tongue of the little mermaid, who now was dumb and could neither sing nor talk.

"If the polyps should pounce on you when you walk back through my wood," the witch said, "just spill a drop of this brew upon them and their tentacles will break in a thousand pieces." But there was no need of that, for the polyps curled up in terror as soon as they saw the bright draught. It glittered in the little mermaid's hand as if it were a shining star. So she soon traversed the forest, the marsh, and the place of raging whirlpools.

She could see her father's palace. The lights had been snuffed out in the great ballroom, and doubtless everyone in the palace was asleep, but she dared not go near them, now that she was stricken dumb and was leaving her home forever. Her heart felt as if it would break with grief. She tip-toed into the garden, took one flower from each of her sisters' little plots, blew a thousand kisses toward the palace, and then mounted up through the dark blue sea.

The sun had not yet risen when she saw the Prince's palace. As she climbed his splendid marble staircase, the moon was shining clear. The little mermaid swallowed the bitter, fiery draught, and it was as if a two-edged sword struck through her frail body. She swooned away, and lay there as if she were dead. When the sun rose over the sea she awoke and felt a flash of pain, but directly in front of her stood the handsome young Prince, gazing at her with his coal-black eyes. Lowering her gaze, she saw that her fish tail was gone, and that she had the loveliest pair of white legs any young maid could hope to have. But she was naked, so she clothed herself in her own long hair.

The Prince asked who she was, and how she came to be there. Her deep blue eyes looked at him tenderly but very sadly, for she could not speak. Then he took her hand

and led her into his palace. Every footstep felt as if she were walking on the blades and points of sharp knives, just as the witch had foretold, but she gladly endured it. She moved as lightly as a bubble as she walked beside the Prince. He and all who saw her marveled at the grace of her gliding walk.

Once clad in the rich silk and muslin garments that were provided for her, she was the loveliest person in all the palace, though she was dumb and could neither sing nor speak. Beautiful slaves, attired in silk and cloth of gold, came to sing before the Prince and his royal parents. One of them sang more sweetly than all the others, and when the Prince smiled at her and clapped his hands, the little mermaid felt very unhappy, for she knew that she herself used to sing much more sweetly. "Oh," she thought, "if he only knew that I parted with my voice forever so that I could be near him." Graceful slaves now began to dance to the most wonderful music. Then the little mermaid lifted her shapely white arms, rose up on the tips of her toes, and skimmed over the floor. No one had ever danced so well. Each movement set off her beauty to better

and better advantage, and her eyes spoke more directly to the heart than any of the singing slaves could do.

She charmed everyone, and especially the Prince, who called her his dear little foundling. She danced time and again, though every time she touched the floor she felt as if she were treading on sharp-edged steel. The Prince said he would keep her with him always, and that she was to have a velvet pillow to sleep on outside his door.

He had a page's suit made for her, so that she could go with him on horseback. They would ride through the sweet scented woods, where the green boughs brushed her shoulders, and where the little birds sang among the fluttering leaves.

She climbed up high mountains with the Prince, and though her tender feet bled so that all could see it, she only laughed and followed him on until they could see the clouds driving far below, like a flock of birds in flight to distant lands.

At home in the Prince's palace, while the others slept at night, she would go down the broad marble steps to cool her burning feet in the cold sea water, and then she would recall those who lived beneath the sea. One night her sisters came by, arm in arm, singing sadly as they breasted the waves.

When she held out her hands toward them, they knew who she was, and told her how unhappy she had made them all. They came to see her every night after that, and once far, far out to sea, she saw her old grandmother, who had not been up to the surface this many a year. With her was the sea king, with his crown upon his head. They stretched out their hands to her, but they did not venture so near the land as her sisters had.

Day after day she became more dear to the Prince, who loved her as one would love a good little child, but he never thought of making her his Queen. Yet she had to be his wife or she would never have an immortal soul, and on the morning after his wedding she would turn into foam on the waves.

"Don't you love me best of all?" the little mermaid's eyes seemed to question him, when he took her in his arms and kissed her lovely forehead.

"Yes, you are most dear to me," said the Prince, "for you have the kindest heart. You love me more than anyone else does, and you look so much like a young girl I once saw but never shall find again. I was on a ship that was wrecked, and the waves cast me ashore near a holy temple, where many young girls performed the rituals. The youngest of them found me beside the sea and saved my life. Though I saw her no more than twice, she is the only person in all the world whom I could love. But you are so much like her that you almost replace the memory of her in my heart. She belongs to that holy temple, therefore it is my

good fortune that I have you. We shall never part."

"Alas, he doesn't know it was I who saved his life," the little mermaid thought. "I carried him over the sea to the garden where the temple stands. I hid behind the foam and watched to see if anyone would come. I saw the pretty maid he loves better than me." A sigh was the only sign of her deep distress, for a mermaid cannot cry. "He says that the other maid belongs to the holy temple. She will never come out into the world, so they will never see each other again. It is I who will care for him, love him, and give all my life to him."

Now rumours arose that the Prince was to wed the beautiful daughter of a neighbouring King, and that it was for this reason he was having such a superb ship made ready to sail. The rumour ran that the Prince's real interest in visiting the neighboring kingdom was to see the King's daughter, and that he was to travel with a lordly retinue. The little mermaid shook her head and smiled, for she knew the Prince's thoughts far better than anyone else did.

"I am forced to make this journey," he told her. "I must visit the beautiful Princess, for this is my parents' wish, but they would not have me bring her home as my bride against my own will, and I can never love her. She does not resemble the lovely maiden in the temple, as you do, and if I were to choose a bride, I would sooner choose you, my dear mute foundling with those telling eyes of yours." And he kissed her on the mouth, fingered her long hair, and laid his head against her heart so that she came to dream of mortal happiness and an immortal soul.

"I trust you aren't afraid of the sea, my silent child ' he said, as they went on board the magnificent vessel that was to carry them to the land of the neighboring King. And he told her stories of storms, of ships becalmed, of strange deep-sea fish, and of the wonders that divers have seen. She smiled at such stories, for no one knew about the bottom of the

sea as well as she did. In the clear moonlight, when everyone except the man at the helm was asleep, she sat on the side of the ship gazing down through the transparent water, and fancied she could catch glimpses of her father's palace. On the topmost tower stood her old grandmother,

wearing her silver crown and looking up at the keel of the ship through the rushing waves. Then her sisters rose to the surface, looked at her sadly, and wrung their white hands. She smiled and waved, trying to let them know that all went well and that she was happy. But along came the cabin boy, and her sisters dived out of sight so quickly that the boy supposed the flash of white he had seen was merely foam on the sea.

Next morning the ship came in to the harbour of the neighboring King's glorious city. All the church bells chimed, and trumpets were sounded from all the high towers, while the soldiers lined up with flying banners and glittering bayonets. Every day had a new festivity, as one ball or levee followed another, but the Princess was still to appear. They said she was being brought up in some far-away sacred temple, where she was learning every royal virtue. But she came at last. The little mermaid was curious to see how beautiful this Princess was, and she had to grant

that a more exquisite figure she had never seen. The Princess's skin was clear and fair, and behind the long, dark lashes her deep blue eyes were smiling and devoted.

"It was you!" the Prince cried. "You are the one who saved me when I lay like a dead man beside the sea." He clasped the blushing bride of his choice in his arms. "Oh, I am happier than a man should be!" he told his little mermaid. "My fondest dream - that which I never dared to hope - has come true. You will share in my great joy, for you love me more than anyone does."

The little mermaid kissed his hand and felt that her heart was beginning to break. For the morning after his wedding day would see her dead and turned to watery foam.

All the church bells rang out, and heralds rode through the streets to announce the wedding. Upon every altar sweet-scented oils were burned in costly silver lamps. The priests swung their censers, the bride and the bridegroom joined their hands, and the bishop blessed their marriage. The little mermaid, clothed in silk and cloth of gold, held the bride's train, but she was deaf to the wedding march and blind to the holy ritual. Her thought turned on her last night upon earth, and on all she had lost in this world.

That same evening, the bride and bridegroom went aboard the ship. Cannon thundered and banners waved. On the deck of the ship a royal pavilion of purple and gold was set up, and furnished with luxurious

cushions. Here the wedded couple were to sleep on that calm, clear night. The sails swelled in the breeze, and the ship glided so lightly that it scarcely seemed to move over the quiet sea. All nightfall brightly coloured lanterns were lighted, and the mariners merrily danced on the deck. The little mermaid could not forget that first time she rose from the depths of the sea and looked on at such pomp and happiness. Light as a swallow pursued by his enemies, she joined in the whirling dance. Everyone cheered her, for never had she danced so wonderfully. Her tender feet felt as if they were pierced by daggers, but she did not feel it. Her heart suffered far greater pain. She knew that this was the last evening that she ever would see him for whom she had forsaken her home and family, for whom she had sacrificed her lovely voice and suffered such constant torment, while he knew nothing of all these things. It was the last night that she would breathe the same air with him, or look upon deep waters or the star fields of the blue sky. A never-ending night, without thought and without dreams, awaited her who had no soul and could not get one. The merrymaking lasted long after midnight, yet she laughed and danced on despite the thought of death she carried in her heart. The Prince kissed his beautiful bride and she toyed with his coal-black hair. Hand in hand, they went to rest in the magnificent pavilion.

A hush came over the ship. Only the helmsman remained on deck as the little mermaid leaned her white arms on the bulwarks and looked to the east to see the first red hint of daybreak, for she knew that the first flash of the sun would strike her dead. Then she saw her sisters rise up among the waves. They were as pale as she, and there was no sign of their

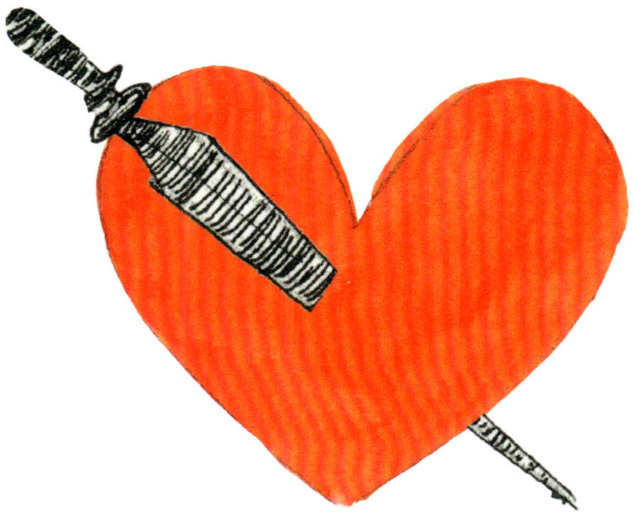

lovely long hair that the breezes used to blow. It had all been cut off.

'We have given our hair to the witch," they said, "so that she would send you help, and save you from death tonight. She gave us a knife. Here it is. See the sharp blade! Before the sun rises, you must strike it into the Prince's heart, and when his warm blood bathes your feet they will grow together and become a fish tail. Then you will be a mermaid again, able to come back to us in the sea, and live out your three hundred years before you die and turn into dead salt sea foam. Make haste! He or you must die before sunrise. Our old grandmother is so grief-stricken that her white hair is falling fast, just as ours did under the witch's scissors. Kill the Prince and come back to us. Hurry! Hurry! See that red glow in the heavens! In a few minutes the sun will rise and you must die." So saying, they gave a strange deep sigh and sank beneath the waves.

The little mermaid parted the purple curtains of the tent and saw the beautiful bride asleep with her head on the Prince's breast. The mermaid bent down and kissed his shapely forehead. She looked at the sky, fast reddening for the break of day. She looked at the sharp knife and again turned her eyes toward the Prince, who in his sleep murmured the name of his bride. His thoughts were all for her, and the knife blade trembled in the mermaid's hand. But then she flung it from her, far out over the waves. Where it fell the waves were red, as if bubbles of blood seethed in the water. With eyes already glazing she looked once more at the Prince, hurled herself over the bulwarks into the sea, and felt her body dissolve in foam.

The sun rose up from the waters. Its beams fell, warm and kindly, upon the chill sea foam, and the little mermaid did not feel the hand of death. In the bright sunlight overhead, she saw hundreds of fair ethereal beings. They were so transparent that through them she could see the ship's white sails and the red clouds in the sky. Their voices were sheer music, but so spirit-like that no human ear could detect the sound, just as no eye on earth could see their forms. Without wings, they floated as light as the air itself. The little mermaid discovered that she was shaped like them, and that she was gradually rising up out of the foam.

'Who are you, toward whom I rise?" she asked, and her voice sounded like those above her, so spiritual that no music on earth could match it.

"We are the daughters of the air," they answered. "A mermaid has no immortal soul, and can never get one unless she wins the love of a human being. Her eternal life must depend upon a power outside herself. The daughters of the air do not have an immortal soul either, but they can earn one by their good deeds. We fly to the south, where the hot poisonous air kills human beings unless we bring cool breezes. We carry the scent of flowers through the air, bringing freshness and healing balm wherever we go. When for three hundred years we have tried to do all the good that we can, we are given an immortal soul and a share in mankind's eternal bliss. You, poor little mermaid, have tried with your whole heart to do this too. Your suffering and your loyalty have raised you up into the realm of airy spirits, and now in the course of three hundred years you may earn by your good deeds a soul that will never die."

# Clumsy Hans

Out in the country there was an old mansion where an old squire lived with his two sons, who were so witty that they thought themselves too clever for words. They decided to go out and propose to the King's daughter, which they were at liberty to do, for she had announced publicly that she would take for a husband the man who had the most to say for himself.

The two brothers made their preparations for eight days beforehand. That was all the time they had, but it was enough, for they had many accomplishments, and everyone knows how useful they can be. One of them knew the whole Latin dictionary by heart and the town's newspaper for three years - so well that he could repeat it backward or forward. The other had learned all the articles of law and knew what every alderman must know; consequently, he was sure he could talk of governmental affairs, and besides this he could embroider suspenders, for he was very gentle and also clever with his fingers.

"I shall win the Princess!" they both said, as their father gave each one of them a beautiful horse. The one who had memorised the dictionary and the newspapers had a coal-black horse, while the one who knew all about governmental affairs and could embroider had a milk-white one. Then they smeared the corners of their mouths with cod-liver oil, to make them more glib.

All the servants assembled in the courtyard to watch them mount their horses, but just then the third brother came up; for there were really three, although nobody paid much attention to the third, because he was

not so learned as the other two. In fact, everybody called him "Clumsy Hans."

"Where are you going in all your Sunday clothes?" he asked.

"To the King's court, to woo the Princess. Haven't you heard what the King's drummer is proclaiming all over the country?" Then they told him about it.

"Gracious," said Clumsy Hans, "I guess I'll go, too!" But his brothers

only burst out laughing at him as they rode away.

"Father," shouted Clumsy Hans, "Let me have a horse. I feel like getting married, too. If she takes me, she takes me; and if she doesn't take me, I'll take her, anyway."

"That's a lot of nonsense!" replied his father. "You'll get no horse from me. Why, you don't know how to talk properly. Now, your brothers are intelligent men."

"If I can't have a horse I'll take the billy goat," said Clumsy Hans. "He belongs to me, and he can carry me very well." So he mounted the billy goat, dug his heels into its sides, and galloped off down the highway.

"Alley-oop! What a ride! Here I come!" shouted Clumsy Hans, singing so loud that his voice was heard far away.

But his two brothers rode quietly on ahead of him. They were not speaking a word to each other, for they were thinking about all the clever speeches they would have to make, and of course these had to be carefully prepared and memorised beforehand.

"Halloo!" cried Clumsy Hans. "Here I come! Look what I found on the road!" Then he showed them a dead crow he had picked up.

"Clumsy!" said the brothers. "What are you going to do with that?"

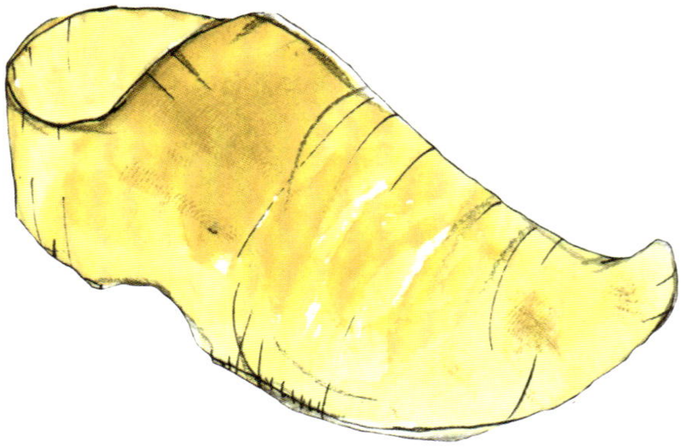

"Why, I am going to give it to the Princess!"

"Yes, you do that," they said as they rode on laughing.

"Halloo, here I come again! Just look what I've found this time! You don't find things like this in the road every day!" So the brothers turned around to see what it was this time.

"Clumsy!" they said. "That's just an old wooden shoe, and the upper part's broken off, anyway. Is the Princess going to have that, too?"

"She certainly is," replied Hans, and the brothers again laughed and rode on far in advance of him.

"Halloo! Here I am again," shouted Clumsy Hans. "Now this is getting better and better! This is really something!"

"Well, what have you found this time?" asked the brothers.

"Oh, I can't really tell you," Clumsy Hans said. "How pleased the Princess will be!"

"Uh!" said the brothers. "Why, it's nothing but mud out of the ditch!"

"Yes, of course," said Clumsy Hans, "but the very finest sort of mud. Look, it runs right through your fingers." Then he filled his pockets with it.

But his brothers galloped on ahead as fast as they could, and so they arrived at the town gate a full hour ahead of Hans. At the gate each suitor was given a numbered ticket, and as fast as they arrived they were arranged in rows, six to a row, packed together so tightly that they could not even move their arms. That was a wise plan, for otherwise they could have cut each other's backs to pieces, just because one stood in front of another. All the inhabitants of the town stood around the castle, peering in through the windows to watch the Princess receive her suitors; but as each young

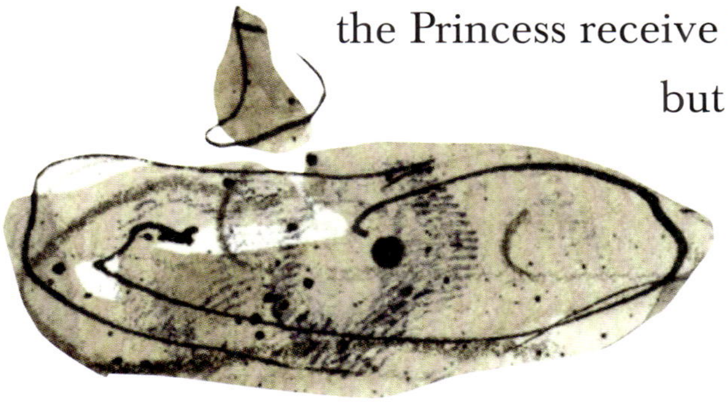

man came into the room, he became tongue-tied.

"No good!" said the Princess. "Take him away!"

Now came the brother who had memorised the dictionary, but he had completely forgotten it while standing in line. The floor creaked under his footsteps, and the ceiling was made of mirrors so that he could see himself standing on his head; and at each window stood three clerks and an alderman, writing down every word that was spoken, so that it immediately could be printed in the newspapers and sold for two pennies on the street corners.

It was a terrible ordeal, and besides there were such fires in the stoves that the pipe was red-hot.

"It's terribly hot in here," said the suitor.

"That's because my father is roasting chickens today," said the Princess.

"Baa!" There he stood. He was not ready for a speech of this kind and hadn't a word to say, just when he wanted to say something extremely witty. "Baa!"

"No good!" said the Princess. "Take him away!" And consequently he had to leave.

Now the second brother approached.

"It's dreadfully warm here," he said.

"Yes, we're roasting chickens today," replied the Princess.

"What-what did you-uh-what?" he stammered, and all the clerks carefully wrote down, "What-what did you-uh-what?"

"No good," said the Princess again. "Out with him!"

Now it was Clumsy Hans's turn, and he rode his billy goat right into the hall.

"Terribly hot in here," he said.

"I'm roasting young chickens," replied the Princess.

"Why, that's fine!" said Clumsy Hans. "Then I suppose I can get my crow roasted?"

"That you can," said the Princess. "But have you anything to roast it in? I haven't any pots or pans." "But I have," replied Clumsy Hans. "Here's a cooking pot with a tin handle!" Then he pulled out the old wooden shoe and put the crow right into it. "Why, that's enough for a whole meal!" said the Princess. "But where do we get the sauce from?"

"I have that in my pocket," replied Clumsy Hans. "In fact, I have so much I can afford to spill some of it." Then he poured a little of the mud from his pocket.

"I like that!" said the Princess. "You have an answer for everything, and you know how to speak. I'll take you for my husband. But do you know that everything we've said and are saying is written down and will be published in the paper tomorrow? Look over there, and you'll see in each window three clerks and an old alderman, and that alderman is the worst of all; he doesn't understand anything!"

She said this only to frighten him, but all the clerks chuckled with delight and spurted blots of ink on the floor.

"Oh, so these are the gentlemen!" said Clumsy Hans. "Then I must give the alderman the best thing I have." Then he turned out his pockets and threw the wet mud in the face of the alderman.

"Cleverly done!" said the Princess. "I could never have done that, but I'll learn in time!"

So Clumsy Hans was made a king, with a wife and a crown, and sat on a throne. And we had this story straight from the alderman's newspaper-but that is one you can't always depend upon.

# Thumbelina

There once was a woman who wanted so very much to have a tiny little child, but she did not know where to find one. So she went to an old witch, and she said:

"I have set my heart upon having a tiny little child. Please could you tell me where I can find one?"

"Why, that's easily done," said the witch. "Here's a grain of barley for you, but it isn't at all the sort of barley that farmers grow in their fields or that the chickens get to eat. Put it in a flower pot and you'll see what you shall see."

"Oh thank you!" the woman said. She gave the witch twelve pennies, and planted the barley seed as soon as she got home. It quickly grew into a fine large flower, which looked very much like a tulip. But the petals were folded tight, as though it were still a bud.

"This is such a pretty flower," said the woman. She kissed its lovely red and yellow petals, and just as she kissed it the flower gave a loud pop! and flew open. It was a tulip, right enough, but on the green cushion in the middle of it sat a tiny girl. She was dainty and fair to see, but she was no taller than your thumb. So she was called Thumbelina.

A nicely polished walnut shell served as her cradle. Her mattress was made of the blue petals of violets, and a rose petal was pulled up to cover her. That was how she slept at night. In the daytime she played on a table where the woman put a plate surrounded with a wreath of flowers. Their stems lay in the water, on which there floated a large tulip petal. Thumbelina used the petal as a boat, and with a pair of white horsehairs for oars she could row clear across the plate - a charming sight. She could sing, too. Her voice was the softest and sweetest that anyone ever has heard.

One night as she lay in her cradle, a horrible toad hopped in through the window. This big, ugly, slimy toad jumped right down on the table where Thumbelina was asleep under the red rose petal.

"Here's a perfect wife for my son!" the toad exclaimed. She seized upon the walnut shell in which Thumbelina lay asleep, and hopped off with it, out the window and into the garden. A big broad stream ran through it, with a muddy marsh along its banks, and here the toad lived with her son. Ugh! he was just like his mother, slimy and horrible. "Co-ax, co-ax, brek-ek-eke-kex," was all that he could say when he saw

the graceful little girl in the walnut shell.

"Don't speak so loud, or you will wake her up," the old toad told him. "She might get away from us yet, for she is as light as a puff of swan's-down. We must put her on one of the broad water lily leaves out in the stream. She is so small and light that it will be just like an island to her, and she can't run away from us while we are making our best room under the mud ready for you two to live in." Many water lilies with broad green leaves grew in the stream, and it looked as if they were floating on the surface. The leaf which lay furthest from the bank was the largest of them all, and it was to this leaf that the old toad swam with the walnut shell which held Thumbelina.

The poor little thing woke up early next morning, and when she saw where she was she began to cry bitterly. There was water all around the big green leaf and there was no way at all for her to reach the shore. The old toad sat in the mud, decorating a room with green rushes and yellow water lilies, to have it looking its best for her new daughter-in-law. Then she and her ugly son swam out to the leaf on which Thumbelina was standing. They came for her pretty little bed, which they wanted to carry to the bridal chamber before they took her there.

The old toad curtsied deep in the water before her, and said:

"Meet my son. He is to be your husband, and you will share a delightful home in the mud."

"Co-ax, co-ax, brek-ek-eke-kex," was all that her son could say.

Then they took the pretty little bed and swam away with it. Left all alone on the green leaf, Thumbelina sat down and cried. She did not want to live in the slimy toad's house, and she didn't want to have the toad's horrible son for her husband. The little fishes who swam in the water beneath her had seen the toad and heard what she had said. So up popped their heads to have a look at the little girl. No sooner had they seen her than they felt very sorry that anyone so pretty should have to go down to live with that hideous toad. No, that should never be! They gathered around the green stem which held the leaf where she was, and gnawed it in two with their teeth. Away went the leaf down the stream, and away went Thumbelina, far away where the toad could not catch her.

Thumbelina sailed past many a place, and when the little birds in the bushes saw her they sang, "What a darling little girl." The leaf drifted further and further away with her, and so it was that Thumbelina became a traveler.

A lovely white butterfly kept fluttering around her, and at last alighted

on the leaf, because he admired Thumbelina. She was a happy little girl again, now that the toad could not catch her. It was all very lovely as she floated along, and where the sun struck the water it looked like shining gold. Thumbelina undid her sash, tied one end of it to the butterfly, and made the other end fast to the leaf. It went much faster now, and Thumbelina went much faster too, for of course she was standing on it.

Just then, a big May-bug flew by and caught sight of her. Immediately he fastened his claws around her slender waist and flew with her up into a tree. Away went the green leaf down the stream, and away went the butterfly with it, for he was tied to the leaf and could not get loose.

My goodness! How frightened little Thumbelina was when the May-bug carried her up in the tree. But she was even more sorry for the nice white butterfly she had fastened to the leaf, because if he couldn't free himself he would have to starve to death. But the May-bug wasn't one to care about that. He sat her down on the largest green leaf of the tree, fed her honey from the flowers, and told her how pretty she was, considering that she didn't look the least like a May-bug. After a while, all the other May-bugs who lived in the tree came to pay them a call. As they stared at Thumbelina, the lady May-bugs threw up their feelers and said:

"Why, she has only two legs-what a miserable sight!"

"She hasn't any feelers," one cried.

"She is pinched in at the waist - how shameful! She looks like a human being - how ugly she is!" said all of the female May-bugs.

Yet Thumbelina was as pretty as ever. Even the May-bug who had flown away with her knew that, but as every last one of them kept calling her ugly, he at length came to agree with them and would have nothing to do with her - she could go wherever she chose. They flew down out of the tree with her and left her on a daisy, where she sat and cried because she was so ugly that the May-bugs wouldn't have anything to do with her.

Nevertheless, she was the loveliest little girl you can imagine, and as frail and fine as the petal of a rose.

All summer long, poor Thumbelina lived all alone in the woods. She wove herself a hammock of grass, and hung it under a big burdock leaf to keep off the rain. She took honey from the flowers for food, and drank the dew which she found on the leaves every morning. In this way the summer and fall went by. Then came the winter, the long, cold winter. All the birds who had sung so sweetly for her flew away. The trees and the flowers withered. The big burdock leaf under which she had lived shriveled up until nothing was left of it but a dry, yellow stalk. She was terribly cold, for her clothes had worn threadbare and she herself was so slender and frail. Poor Thumbelina, she would freeze to death! Snow began to fall, and every time a snowflake struck her it was as if she had been hit by a whole shovelful, for we are quite tall while she measured only an inch. She wrapped a withered leaf about her, but there was no warmth in it. She shivered with cold.

Near the edge of the woods where she now had arrived, was a large grain field, but the grain had

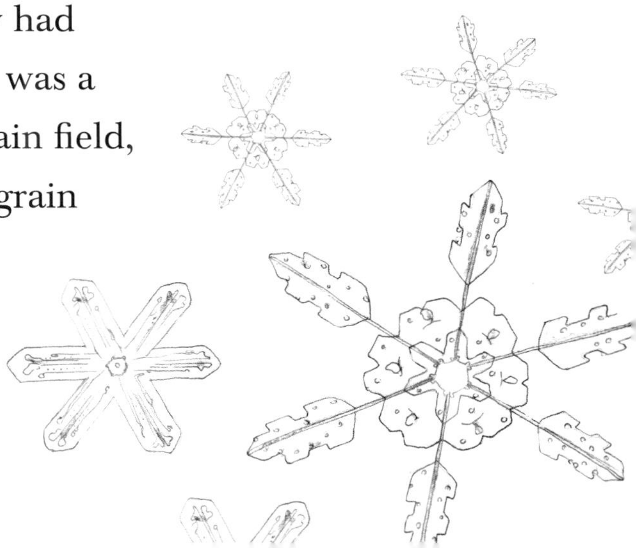

harvested long ago. Only the dry, bare stubble stuck out of the frozen ground. It was just as if she were lost in a vast forest, and oh how she shivered with cold! Then she came to the door of a field mouse, who had a little hole amidst the stubble. There this mouse lived, warm and cozy, with a whole store-room of grain, and a magnificent kitchen and pantry. Poor Thumbelina stood at the door, just like a beggar child, and pled for a little bit of barley, because she hadn't had anything to eat for two days past.

"Why, you poor little thing," said the field mouse, who turned out to be a kind-hearted old creature. "You must come into my warm room and share my dinner."

She took such a fancy to Thumbelina that she said, "If you care to, you may stay with me all winter, but you must keep my room tidy, and tell me stories, for I am very fond of them." Thumbelina did as the kind old field mouse asked and she had a very good time of it.

"Soon we shall have a visitor," the field mouse said. "Once every week my neighbour comes to see me, and he is even better off than I am. His rooms are large, and he wears such a beautiful black velvet coat. If you could only get him for a husband you would be well taken care of, but he can't see anything. You must tell him the very best stories you know."

Thumbelina did not like this suggestion. She would not even consider the neighbour, because

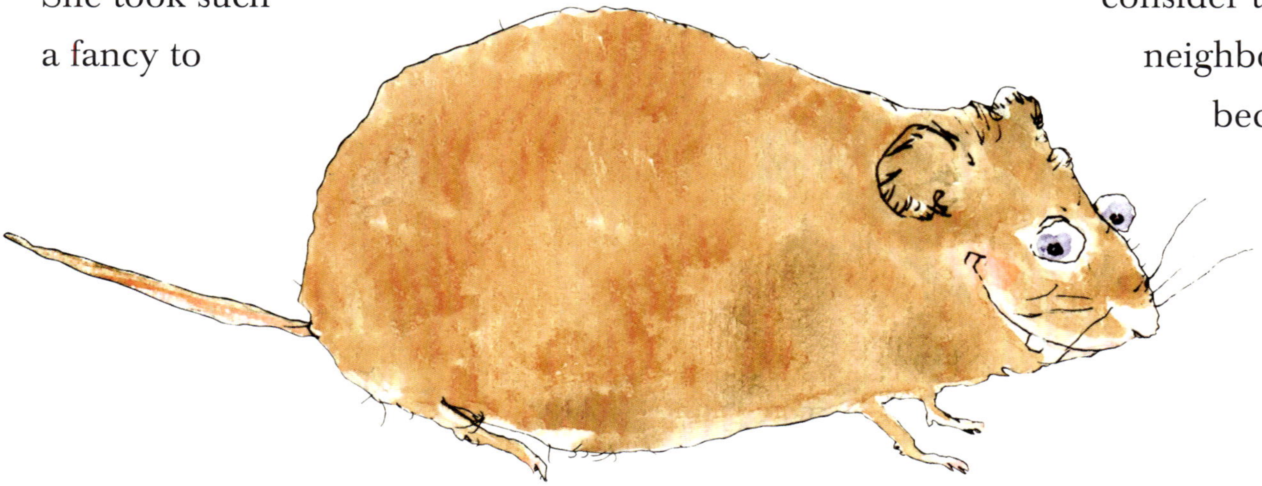

he was a mole. He paid them a visit in his black velvet coat. The field mouse talked about how wealthy and wise he was, and how his home was more than twenty times larger than hers. But for all of his knowledge he cared nothing at all for the sun and the flowers. He had nothing good to say for them, and had never laid eyes on them. As Thumbelina had to sing for him, she sang, "May-bug, May-bug, fly away home," and "The Monk goes afield." The mole fell in love with her sweet voice, but he didn't say anything about it yet, for he was a most discreet fellow.

He had just dug a long tunnel through the ground from his house to theirs, and the field mouse and Thumbelina were invited to use it whenever they pleased, though he warned them not to be alarmed by the dead bird which lay in this passage. It was a complete bird, with feather and beak. It must have died quite recently, when winter set in, and it was buried right in the middle of the tunnel.

The mole took in his mouth a torch of decayed wood. In the darkness it glimmered like fire. He went ahead of them to light the way through the long, dark passage. When they came to where the dead bird lay, the mole put his broad nose to the ceiling and made a large hole through which daylight could fall. In the middle of the floor lay a dead swallow, with his lovely wings folded at his sides and his head tucked under his feathers.

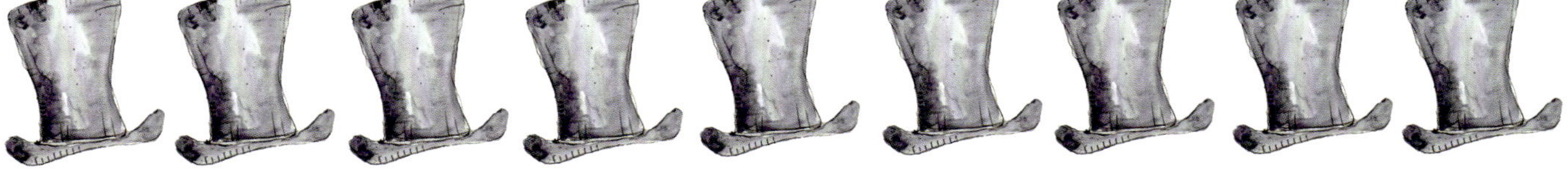

The poor bird must certainly have died of the cold. Thumbelina felt so sorry for him. She loved all the little birds who had sung and sweetly twittered to her all through the summer. But the mole gave the body a kick with his short stumps, and said, "Now he won't be chirping any more. What a wretched thing it is to be born a little bird. Thank goodness none of my children can be a bird, who has nothing but his 'chirp, chirp', and must starve to death when winter comes along."

"Yes, you are so right, you sensible man," the field mouse agreed. "What good is all his chirp-chirping to a bird in the winter time, when he starves and freezes? But that's considered very grand, I imagine."

Thumbelina kept silent, but when the others turned their back on the bird she bent over, smoothed aside the feathers that hid the bird's head, and kissed his closed eyes. "Maybe it was he who sang so sweetly to me in the summertime," she thought to herself. "What pleasure he gave me, the dear, pretty bird."

The mole closed up the hole that let in the daylight, and then he took the ladies home. That night Thumbelina could not sleep a wink, so she got up and wove a fine large coverlet out of hay. She took it to the dead bird and spread it over him, so that he would lie warm in the cold earth. She tucked him in with some soft thistledown that she had found in the field mouse's room.

"Good-by, you pretty little bird," she said. "Good-by, and thank you for your sweet songs last summer, when the trees were all green and the sun shone so warmly upon us." She laid her head on his breast, and it startled her to feel a soft thump, as if something were beating inside. This was the bird's heart. He was not dead-he was only numb with cold, and now that he had been warmed he came to life again.

In the fall, all swallows fly off to warm countries, but if one of them starts too late he gets so cold that he drops down as if he were dead, and lies where he fell. And then the cold snow covers him.

Thumbelina was so frightened that she trembled, for the bird was so big, so enormous compared to her own inch of height. But she mustered her courage, tucked the cotton wool down closer around the poor bird, brought the mint leaf that covered her own bed, and spread it over the bird's head.

The following night she tiptoed out to him again. He was alive now, but so weak that he could barely open his eyes for a moment to look at Thumbelina, who stood beside him with the piece of touchwood that was her only lantern.

"Thank you, pretty little child," the sick swallow said. "I have been wonderfully warmed. Soon I shall get strong once more, and be able to fly again in the warm sunshine."

"Oh," she said, "It's cold outside, it's snowing, and freezing. You just

stay in your warm bed and I'll nurse you."

Then she brought him some water in the petal of a flower. The swallow drank, and told her how he had hurt one of his wings in a thorn bush, and for that reason couldn't fly as fast as the other swallows when they flew far, far away to the warm countries. Finally he had dropped to the ground. That was all he remembered, and he had no idea how he came to be where she found him. The swallow stayed there all through the winter, and Thumbelina was kind to him and tended him with loving care. She didn't say anything about this to the field mouse or to the mole, because they did not like the poor unfortunate swallow.

As soon as spring came and the sun warmed the earth, the swallow told Thumbelina it was time to say good-by. She reopened the hole that the mole had made in the ceiling, and the sun shone in splendor upon them. The swallow asked Thumbelina to go with him. She could sit on his back as they flew away through the green woods. But Thumbelina knew that it would make the old field mouse feel badly if she left like that, so she said:

"No, I cannot go."

"Fare you well, fare you well, my good and pretty girl," said the swallow, as he flew into the sunshine. Tears came into Thumbelina's eyes as she watched him go, for she was so fond of the poor swallow.

"Chirp, chirp!" sang the bird, at he flew into the green woods. Thumbelina felt very downcast. She was not permitted to go out in the warm sunshine. Moreover, the grain that was sown in the field above the field mouse's house grew so tall that, to a poor little girl who was only an inch high, it was like a dense forest.

"You must work on your trousseau this summer," the field mouse said, for their neighbor, that loathsome mole in his black velvet coat, had proposed to her. "You must have both woolens and linens, both bedding and wardrobe, when you become the mole's wife."

Thumbelina had to turn the spindle, and the field mouse hired four spiders to spin and weave for her day and night. The mole came to call every evening, and his favourite remark was that the sun, which now baked the earth as hard as a rock, would not be nearly so hot when summer was over. Yes, as soon as summer was past he would be marrying Thumbelina. But she was not at all happy about it, because she didn't like the tedious mole the least bit. Every morning at sunrise and every evening at sunset, she would steal out the door. When the breeze blew the ears of grain apart she could catch glimpses of the blue sky. She could dream about how bright and fair it was out of doors, and how she wished she would see her dear swallow again. But he did not come back, for doubtless he was far away, flying about in the lovely green woods.

When fall arrived, Thumbelina's whole trousseau was ready.

"Your wedding day is four weeks off," the field mouse told her. But Thumbelina cried and declared that she would not have the tedious mole for a husband.

"Fiddlesticks," said the field mouse. "Don't you be obstinate, or I'll bite you with my white teeth. Why, you're getting a superb husband. The queen herself hasn't a black velvet coat as fine as his. Both his kitchen and his cellar are well supplied. You ought to thank goodness that you are getting him."

Then came the wedding day. The mole had come to take Thumbelina home with him, where she would have to live deep underground and never go out in the warm sunshine again, because he disliked it so. The poor little girl felt very sad that she had to say good-by to the glorious sun, which the field mouse had at least let her look out at through the doorway.

"Farewell, bright sun!" she said. With her arm stretched toward it she walked a little way from the field mouse's home. The grain had been harvested, and only the dry stubble was left in the field. "Farewell. farewell!" she cried again, and flung her little arms around a small red flower that was still in bloom. "If you see my dear swallow, please give him my love."

"Chirp, chirp! Chirp, chirp!" She suddenly heard a twittering over her head. She looked up and there was the swallow, just passing by. He was so glad to see Thumbelina although, when she told him how she hated to marry the mole and live deep underground where the sun never shone, she could not hold back her tears.

"Now that the cold winter is coming," the swallow told her, "I shall fly far, far away to the warm countries. Won't you come along with me? You can ride on my back. Just tie yourself on with your sash, and away we'll fly, far from the ugly mole and his dark hole-far, far away, over the mountains to the warm countries where the sun shines so much fairer than here, to where it is always summer and there are always flowers. Please fly away with me, dear little Thumbelina, you who saved my life when I lay frozen in a dark hole in the earth."

"Yes, I will go with you!" said Thumbelina. She sat on his back, put her feet on his outstretched wings, and fastened her sash to one of his strongest feathers. Then the swallow soared into the air over forests and over lakes, high up over the great mountains that are always capped

with snow. When Thumbelina felt cold in the chill air, she crept under the bird's warm feathers, with only her little head stuck out to watch all the wonderful sights below. At length they came to the warm countries. There the sun shone far more brightly than it ever does here, and the sky seemed twice as high. Along the ditches and hedgerows grew marvelous green and blue grapes. Lemons and oranges hung in the woods. The air smelled sweetly of myrtle and thyme. By the wayside, the loveliest children ran hither and thither, playing with the brightly coloured butterflies. But the swallow flew on still farther, and it became more and more beautiful. Under magnificent green trees, on the

shore of a blue lake there stood an ancient palace of dazzling white marble. The lofty pillars were wreathed with vines, and at the top of them many swallows had made their nests. One nest belonged to the swallow who carried Thumbelina.

"This is my home," the swallow told her. "If you will choose one of those glorious flowers in bloom down below, I shall place you in it, and you will have all that your heart desires."

"That will be lovely," she cried, and clapped her tiny hands.

A great white marble pillar had fallen to the ground, where it lay in three broken pieces. Between these pieces grew the loveliest large white flowers. The swallow flew down with Thumbelina and put her on one of the large petals. How surprised she was to find in the center of the flower a little man, as shining and transparent as if he had been made of glass. On his head was the daintiest of little gold crowns, on his shoulders were the brightest shining wings, and he was not a bit bigger than Thumbelina. He was the spirit of the flower. In every flower there lived a small man or woman just like him, but he was the king over all of them.

"Oh, isn't he handsome?" Thumbelina said softly to the swallow. The king was somewhat afraid of the swallow, which seemed a very giant of a bird to anyone as small as he. But when he saw Thumbelina he rejoiced, for she was the prettiest little girl he had ever laid eyes on. So he took off his golden crown and put it on her head. He asked if he might know her name, and he asked her to be his wife, which would make her queen over all the flowers. Here indeed was a different sort of

husband from the toad's son and the mole with his black velvet coat. So she said "Yes" to this charming king. From all the flowers trooped little ladies and gentlemen delightful to behold. Every one of them brought Thumbelina a present, but the best gift of all was a pair of wings that had belonged to a large silver fly. When these were made fast to her back, she too could flit from flower to flower. Everyone rejoiced, as the swallow perched above them in his nest and sang his very best songs for them. He was sad though, deep down in his heart, for he liked Thumbelina so much that he wanted never to part with her.

"Good-by, good-by," said the swallow. He flew away again from the warm countries, back to far-away Denmark, where he had a little nest over the window of the man who can tell you fairy tales. To him the bird sang, "Chirp, chirp! Chirp, chirp!" and that's how we heard the whole story.

# The Little Match Girl

It was so terribly cold. Snow was falling, and it was almost dark. Evening came on, the last evening of the year. In the cold and gloom a poor little girl, bareheaded and barefoot, was walking through the streets. Of course when she had left her house she'd had slippers on, but what good had they been? They were very big slippers, way too big for her, for they belonged to her mother. The little girl had lost them running across the road, where two carriages had rattled by terribly fast. One slipper she'd not been able to find again, and a boy had run off with the other, saying he could use it very well as a cradle some day when he had children of his own.

And so the little girl walked on her naked feet, which were quite red and blue with the cold. In an old apron she carried several packages of matches, and she held a box of them in her hand. No one had bought any from her all day long, and no one had given her a cent.

Shivering with cold and hunger, she crept along, a picture of misery, poor little girl! The snowflakes fell on her long fair hair, which hung in pretty curls over her neck. In all the windows lights were shining, and there was a wonderful smell of roast goose, for it was New Year's eve. Yes, she thought of that!

In a corner formed by two houses, one of which projected farther out into the street than the other, she sat down and drew up her little feet under her. She was getting colder and colder, but did not dare to go home, for she had sold no matches, nor earned a single cent, and her father would surely beat her. Besides, it was cold at home, for they had nothing over them but a roof through which the wind whistled even though the biggest cracks had been stuffed with straw and rags.

Her hands were almost dead with cold. Oh, how much one little match might warm her! If she could only take one from the box and rub it against the wall and warm her hands. She drew one out. R-r-ratch! How it sputtered and burned! It made a warm, bright flame, like a little candle, as she held her hands over it; but it gave a strange light! It really seemed to the little girl as if she were sitting before a great iron stove with shining brass knobs and a brass cover. How wonderfully the fire burned! How comfortable it was! The youngster stretched out her feet to warm them too; then the little flame went out, the stove vanished, and she had only the remains of the burnt match in her hand. She struck another match against the wall. It burned brightly, and when the light fell upon the wall it became transparent like a thin veil, and she could see through it into a room. On the table a snow-white cloth was spread, and on it stood a shining dinner service. The roast goose steamed gloriously, stuffed with apples and prunes. And what was still better, the goose jumped down from the dish and waddled along the floor with a knife and fork

in its breast, right over to the little girl. Then the match went out, and she could see

only the thick, cold wall. She lighted another match. Then she was sitting under the most beautiful Christmas tree. It was much larger and much more beautiful than the one she had seen last Christmas through the glass door at the rich merchant's home. Thousands of candles burned on the green branches, and colored pictures like those in the printshops looked down at her. The little girl reached both her hands toward them. Then the match went out. But the Christmas lights mounted higher. She saw them now as bright stars in the sky. One of them fell down, forming a long line of fire.

"Now someone is dying," thought the little girl, for her old grandmother, the only person who had loved her, and who was now dead, had told her that when a star fell down a soul went up to God.

She rubbed another match against the wall. It became bright again, and in the glow the old grandmother stood clear and shining, kind and lovely.

"Grandmother!" cried the child. "Oh, take me with you! I know you will disappear when the match is burned out. You will vanish like the warm stove, the wonderful roast goose and the beautiful big Christmas tree!"

And she quickly struck the whole bundle of matches, for she wished to keep her grandmother with her. And the matches burned with such a glow that it became brighter than daylight. Grandmother had never been so grand and beautiful. She took the little girl in her arms, and both of them flew in brightness and joy above the earth, very, very high, and up there was neither cold, nor hunger, nor fear - they were with God. But in the corner, leaning against the wall, sat the little girl with red cheeks and smiling mouth, frozen to death on the last evening of the old year. The New Year's sun rose upon a little pathetic figure. The child sat there, stiff and cold, holding the matches, of which one bundle was almost burned.

"She wanted to warm herself," the people said. No one imagined what beautiful things she had seen, and how happily she had gone with her old grandmother into the bright New Year.

# The Nightingale

It's been a great many years since this story happened in China, but that's all the more reason for telling it before it gets forgotten.

The Emperor of China´s palace was the wonder of the world. It was made entirely of fine porcelain, extremely expensive but so delicate that you could touch it only with the greatest of care. In the garden the rarest flowers bloomed, and to the prettiest ones were tied little silver bells which tinkled so that no one could pass by without noticing them. Yes, all things were arranged according to plan in the Emperor's garden, though how far and wide it extended not even the gardener knew. If you walked on and on, you came to a fine forest where the trees were tall and the lakes were deep. The forest ran down to the deep blue sea, so close that tall ships could sail under the branches of the trees. In these trees a nightingale lived. His song was so ravishing that even the poor fisherman, who had much else to do, stopped to listen on the nights when he went out to cast his nets, and heard the nightingale.

"How beautiful that is," he said, but he had his work to attend to, and he would forget the bird's song. But the next night, when he heard the song he would again say, "How beautiful."

From all the countries in the world travelers came to the city of the Emperor. They admired the city. They admired the palace and its garden, but when they heard the nightingale they said, "That is the best of all."

And the travelers told of it when they came home, and men of learning wrote many books about the town, about the palace, and about the garden. But they did not forget the nightingale. They praised him highest of all, and those who were poets wrote magnificent poems about the nightingale who lived in the forest by the deep sea. These books went all the world over, and some of them came even to the Emperor of

China. He sat in his golden chair and read, nodding his head in delight over such glowing descriptions of his city, and palace, and garden. But the nightingale is the best of all. He read it in print.

"What's this?" the Emperor exclaimed. "I don't know of any nightingale. Can there be such a bird in my empire-in my own garden-and I not know it? To think that I should have to learn of it out of a book."

Thereupon he called his Lord-in-Waiting, who was so exalted that when anyone of lower rank dared speak to him, or ask him a question, he only answered, "P", which means nothing at all.

"They say there's a most remarkable bird called the nightingale," said the Emperor. "They say it's the best thing in all my empire. Why haven't I been told about it?"

"I've never heard the name mentioned," said the Lord-in-Waiting. "He hasn't been presented at court." "I command that he appear before me this evening, and sing," said the Emperor. "The whole world knows my possessions better than I do!"

"I never heard of him before," said the Lord-in-Waiting. "But I shall look for him. I'll find him."

But where? The Lord-in-Waiting ran upstairs and downstairs, through all the rooms and corridors, but no one he met with had ever heard tell of the nightingale. So the Lord-in-Waiting ran back to the Emperor, and said it must be a story invented by those who write books.

"Your Imperial Majesty would scarcely believe how much of what is written is fiction, if not downright black art."

"But the book I read was sent me by the mighty Emperor of Japan," said the Emperor. "Therefore it can't be a pack of lies. I must hear this nightingale. I insist upon his being here this evening. He has my high imperial favor, and if he is not forthcoming I will have the whole court punched in the stomach, directly after supper."

"Tsing-pe!" said the Lord-in-Waiting, and off he scurried up the stairs, through all the rooms and corridors. And half the court ran with him, for no one wanted to be punched in the stomach after supper.

There was much questioning as to the whereabouts of this remarkable nightingale, who was so well known everywhere in the world except at home. At last they found a poor little kitchen girl, who said:

"The nightingale? I know him well. Yes, indeed he can sing. Every evening I get leave to carry scraps from table to my sick mother. She lives down by the shore. When I start back I am tired, and rest in the woods. Then I hear the nightingale sing. It brings tears to my

eyes. It's as if my mother were kissing me."

"Little kitchen girl," said the Lord-in-Waiting, "I'll have you appointed scullion for life. I'll even get permission for you to watch the Emperor dine, if you'll take us to the nightingale who is commanded to appear at court this evening."

So they went into the forest where the nightingale usually sang. Half the court went along. On the way to the forest a cow began to moo.

"Oh," cried a courtier, "that must be it. What a powerful voice for a creature so small. I'm sure I've heard her sing before."

"No, that's the cow mooing," said the little kitchen girl. "We still have a long way to go."

Then the frogs in the marsh began to croak.

"Glorious!" said the Chinese court person. "Now I hear it - like church bells ringing."

"No, that's the frogs," said the little kitchen girl. "But I think we shall hear him soon."

Then the nightingale sang.

"That's it," said the little kitchen girl. "Listen, listen! And yonder he sits." She pointed to a little gray bird high up in the branches.

"Is it possible?" cried the Lord-in Waiting. "Well, I never would have thought he looked like that, so unassuming. But he has probably turned pale at seeing so many important people around him."

"Little nightingale," the kitchen girl called to him, "our gracious Emperor wants to hear you sing."

"With the greatest of pleasure," answered the nightingale, and burst into song.

"Very similar to the sound of glass bells," said the Lord-in-Waiting. "Just see his little throat, how busily it throbs. I'm astounded that we have never heard him before. I'm sure he'll be a great success at court." "Shall I sing to the Emperor again?" asked the nightingale, for he thought that the Emperor was present.

"My good little nightingale," said the Lord-in-Waiting, "I have the honor to command your presence at a court function this evening, where you'll delight His Majesty the Emperor with your charming song."

"My song sounds best in the woods," said the nightingale, but he went with them willingly when he heard it was the Emperor's wish.

The palace had been especially polished for the occasion. The porcelain walls and floors shone in the rays of many gold lamps. The flowers with tinkling bells on them had been brought into the halls,

and there was such a commotion of coming and going that all the bells chimed away until you could scarcely hear yourself talk.

In the middle of the great throne room, where the Emperor sat, there was a golden perch for the nightingale. The whole court was there, and they let the little kitchen girl stand behind the door, now that she had been appointed "Imperial Pot-Walloper." Everyone was dressed in his best, and all stared at the little grey bird to which the Emperor graciously nodded.

And the nightingale sang so sweetly that tears came into the Emperor's eyes and rolled down his cheeks. Then the nightingale sang still more sweetly, and it was the Emperor's heart that melted. The Emperor was so touched that he wanted his own golden slipper hung round the nightingale's neck, but the nightingale declined it with thanks. He had already been amply rewarded.

"I have seen tears in the Emperor's eyes," he said. "Nothing could surpass that. An Emperor's tears are strangely powerful. I have my reward." And he sang again, gloriously.

"It's the most charming coquetry we ever heard," said the ladies-in-waiting. And they took water in their mouths so they could gurgle when anyone spoke to them, hoping to rival the nightingale. Even the lackeys and chambermaids said they were satisfied, which was saying a great deal, for they were the hardest to please. Unquestionably the nightingale was a success. He was to stay at court, and have his own cage. He had permission to go for a walk twice a day, and once a night. Twelve footmen attended him, each one holding tight to a ribbon tied to the bird's leg. There wasn't much fun in such outings.

The whole town talked about the marvelous bird, and if two people met, one could scarcely say "night" before the other said "gale," and then they would sigh in unison, with no need for words. Eleven pork-butchers' children were named "nightingale," but not one could sing. One day the Emperor received a large package labeled "The Nightingale."

"This must be another book about my celebrated bird," he said. But it was not a book. In the box was a work of art, an artificial nightingale most like the real one except that it was encrusted with diamonds, rubies and sapphires. When it was wound, the artificial bird could sing one of the nightingale's songs while it wagged its glittering gold and silver tail. Round its neck hung a ribbon inscribed: "The Emperor of Japan's nightingale is a poor thing compared with that of the Emperor of China."

"Isn't that nice?" everyone said, and the man who had brought the contraption was immediately promoted to be "Imperial-Nightingale-Fetcher-in-Chief."

"Now let's have them sing together. What a duet that will be," said the courtiers.

So they had to sing together, but it didn't turn out so well, for the real nightingale sang whatever came into

his head while the imitation bird sang by rote.

"That's not the newcomer's fault," said the music master. "He keeps perfect time, just as I have taught him."

Then they had the imitation bird sing by itself. It met with the same success as the real nightingale, and besides it was much prettier to see, all sparkling like bracelets and breastpins. Three and thirty times it sang the selfsame song without tiring. The courtiers would gladly have heard it again, but the Emperor said the real nightingale should now have his turn. Where was he? No one had noticed him flying out the open window, back to his home in the green forest.

"But what made him do that?" said the Emperor.

All the courtiers slandered the nightingale, whom they called a most ungrateful wretch. "Luckily we have the best bird," they said, and made the imitation one sing again. That was the thirty-fourth time they had heard the same tune, but they didn't quite know it by heart because it was a difficult piece. And the music master praised the artificial bird beyond measure. Yes, he said that the contraption was much better than the real nightingale, not only in its dress and its many beautiful diamonds, but also in its mechanical interior.

"You see, ladies and gentlemen, and above all Your Imperial Majesty, with a real nightingale one never knows what to expect, but with this artificial bird everything goes according to plan. Nothing is left to chance. I can explain it and take it to pieces, and show how the mechanical wheels are arranged, how they go around, and how one follows after another."

"Those are our sentiments exactly," said they all, and the music master was commanded to have the bird give a public concert next Sunday. The Emperor said that his people should hear it. And hear it they did! Everyone said, "Oh," and held up the finger we call "lickpot," and nodded his head. But the poor fishermen who had heard the real nightingale said, "This is very pretty, very nearly the real thing, but not quite. I can't imagine what's lacking."

The real nightingale had been banished from the land. In its place, the artificial bird sat on a cushion beside the Emperor's bed. All its gold and jeweled presents lay about it, and its title was now "Grand Imperial Singer-of-the-Emperor-to-sleep." In rank it stood first from the left, for the Emperor gave preëminence to the left side because of the heart. Even an Emperor's heart is on the left.

The music master wrote a twenty-five-volume book about the artificial bird. It was learned, long-winded, and full of hard Chinese words, yet everybody said they read and understood it, lest they show themselves stupid and would then have been punched in their stomachs.

After a year the Emperor, his court, and all of China knew every twitter of the artificial song by heart. They liked it all the better now that they could sing it themselves. Which they did. The street urchins sang,

"Zizizi! kluk, kluk, kluk," and the Emperor sang it too. That's how popular it was.

But one night, while the artificial bird was singing his best by the Emperor's bed, something inside the bird broke with a twang. Whir-r-r, all the wheels ran down and the music stopped. Out of bed jumped the Emperor and sent for his own physician, but what could he do? Then he sent for a watchmaker, who conferred, and investigated, and patched up the bird after a fashion. But the watchmaker said that the bird must be spared too much exertion, for the cogs were badly worn and if he replaced them it would spoil the tune. This was terrible. Only once a year could they let the bird sing, and that was almost too much for it. But the music master made a little speech full of hard Chinese words which meant that the bird was as good as it ever was. So that made it as good as ever.

Five years passed by, and a real sorrow befell the whole country. The people of China loved their Emperor, and now he fell ill. Ill unto death, it was said. A new Emperor was chosen in readiness. People stood in the palace street and asked the Lord-in-Waiting how it went with their Emperor.

"P," said he, and shook his head.

Cold and pale lay the Emperor in his great magnificent bed. All the courtiers thought he was dead, and went to do homage to the new Emperor. The lackeys went off to trade gossip, and the chambermaids gave a coffee party because it was such a special occasion. Deep mats were laid in all the rooms and passageways, to muffle each footstep. It was quiet in the palace, dead quiet. But the Emperor was not yet dead. Stiff and pale he lay, in his magnificent bed with the long velvet curtains and the heavy gold tassels. High in the wall was an open window, through which moonlight fell on the Emperor and his artificial bird.

The poor Emperor could hardly breathe. It was as if something were sitting on his chest. Opening his eyes he saw it was Death who sat there, wearing the Emperor's crown, handling the Emperor's gold sword, and carrying the Emperor's silk banner. Among the folds of the great velvet curtains there were strangely familiar faces. Some were horrible, others gentle and kind. They were the Emperor's deeds, good and bad, who

came back to him now that Death sat on his heart.

"Don't you remember-?" they whispered one after the other. "Don't you remember-?" And they told him of things that made the cold sweat run on his forehead.

"No, I will not remember!" said the Emperor. "Music, music, sound the great drum of China lest I hear what they say!" But they went on whispering, and Death nodded, at every word.

"Music, music!" the Emperor called. "Sing, my precious little golden bird, sing! I have given you gold and precious presents. I have hung my golden slipper around your neck. Sing, I pray you, sing!"

But the bird stood silent. There was no one to wind it, nothing to make it sing. Death kept staring through his great hollow eyes, and it was quiet, deadly quiet.

Suddenly, through the window came a burst of song. It was the little live nightingale who sat outside on a spray. He had heard of the Emperor's plight, and had come to sing of comfort and hope. As he sang, the phantoms grew pale, and still more pale, and the blood flowed quicker and quicker through the Emperor's feeble body. Even Death listened, and said, "Go on, little nightingale, go on!"

"But," said the little nightingale, "will you give back that sword, that banner, that Emperor's crown?"

And Death gave back these treasures for a song. The nightingale sang on. It sang of the quiet churchyard where white roses grow, where the elder flowers make the air sweet, and where the grass is always green, wet with the tears of those who are still alive. Death longed for his garden. Out through the windows drifted a cold grey mist, as Death departed.

"Thank you, thank you!" the Emperor said. "Little bird from Heaven, I know you of old. I banished you once from my land, and yet you have sung away the evil faces from my bed, and Death from my heart. How can I repay you?" "You have already rewarded me," said the nightingale. "I brought tears to your eyes when first I sang for you. To the heart of a singer those are more precious than any precious stone. But sleep now, and grow fresh and strong while I sing." He sang on until the Emperor fell into a sound, refreshing sleep, a sweet and soothing slumber.

The sun was shining in his window when the Emperor awoke, restored and well. Not one of his servants had returned to him, for they thought him dead, but the nightingale still sang.

"You must stay with me always," said the

Emperor. "Sing to me only when you please. I shall break the artificial bird into a thousand pieces."

"No," said the nightingale. "It did its best. Keep it near you. I cannot build my nest here, or live in a palace, so let me come as I will. Then I shall sit on the spray by your window, and sing things that will make you happy and thoughtful too. I'll sing about those who are gay, and those who are sorrowful. My songs will tell you of all the good and evil that you do not see. A little singing bird flies far and wide, to the fisherman's hut, to the farmer's home, and to many other places a long way off from you and your court. I love your heart better than I do your crown, and yet the crown has been blessed too. I will come and sing to you, if you will promise me one thing."

"All that I have is yours," cried the Emperor, who stood in his imperial robes, which he had put on himself, and held his heavy gold sword to his heart.

"One thing only," the nightingale asked. "You must not let anyone know that you have a little bird who tells you everything; then all will go even better." And away he flew.

The servants came in to look after their dead Emperor and there they stood. And the Emperor said, "Good morning."